Sanity, Insanity,
and Common
Sense

Sanity, Insanity, and Common Sense

RICK SUAREZ, Ph.D.

ROGER C. MILLS, Ph.D.

DARLENE STEWART, M.S.

Fawcett Columbine • New York

Grateful acknowledgment is made to the following for permission to reprint previously published material:

American Association for the Advancement of Science: excerpts from "The Shrinking of George" by Perry Turner which appeared in the June issue of *Science '86*, Vol. 7, No. 5. Copyright © 1986 by the American Association for the Advancement of Science. Reprinted by permission.

American Psychological Association: excerpts from an article entitled "The Psychologist as an Expert Witness on the Issue of Insanity" by Ray Jeffrey which appeared in *American Psychologist*, 1964. Copyright © 1964 by the American Psychological Association. Reprinted by permission of the publisher.

Library of Congress Cataloging-in-Publication Data

Suarez, E. M. (Enrique M.)
Sanity, insanity, and common sense.

Includes index.
1. Psychotherapy, Brief. 2. Mental health. 3. Psychology—Popular works. I. Mills, Roger C. II. Stewart, Darlene, 1937– . III. Title. RC480.55.S84 1987   616.89   86-32067
ISBN 0-449-90244-7

Design by Holly Johnson
Manufactured in the United States of America

First Ballantine Books Edition: June 1987
10   9   8   7   6   5   4   3   2   1

We dedicate this book to the many people who have assisted us in our professional work and who trusted our "hunches" about the direction that led to the discoveries presented in this book. We want to thank all of the people who stayed with us as we began to shift our direction away from the traditional formulations within psychology to tread on new ground. These people provided support and encouragement that helped us far beyond what they realize.

We also thank our "natural" teachers, the people who exhibit common sense in their lives to a degree far beyond what we are able to learn from any textbook. It was their wisdom, natural enjoyment in life, and beauty that initially triggered our inquiries.

CONTENTS

INTRODUCTION

As is often the case, the story behind the publication of *Sanity, Insanity, and Common Sense* is a book in itself. Yet, the reason that this book was written can be summed up in one simple word whose meaning has eluded the grasp of the psychologist: change. In 1977, I was a practicing psychologist who had worked in large neuropsychiatric, rehabilitation, and medical-surgical hospital settings. In the three years since I had received my doctoral degree in psychology, I had, with all the enthusiasm of a new "doctor," applied the traditional techniques of psychotherapy that I had been taught would help people who were suffering psychologically. To the best of my ability, I would dissect people's problems, review their pasts with a fine-tooth comb, paint a picture of their personalities, and finally get them to accept this picture as reflecting their true identity. I would then attempt to change the picture that I myself had painted and that they had accepted. This was the process called psychotherapy.

Psychotherapy! This was where I began to lose my enthusiasm. Psychotherapy dictated that I try to help unhappy, tormented, and often desperate people find their sanity by recalling and reliving their past or present traumas, encouraging them to get in touch with, confront and express what I believed were their repressed fears, angers, or anxieties. In many cases, I required my patients to rehearse what I thought was sane behavior and practice rituals at home to help them cope with their lives. In some severe cases, I would resort to the use of electronic equipment to administer painful electric shocks in an attempt to eradicate maladaptive behavioral habits. Many of my patients vehemently resisted these treatments, but because I was the doctor—the expert—the vast majority would eventually comply and submit to my treatment.

Although I was a technically competent psychotherapist, there

Introduction

was always an unwelcomed fact in my reality as a psychologist that I could never fully ignore. I had never seen anyone really become mentally healthy as a result of my treatments. What I had seen were people who would become dependent on me or a ritual that I had convinced them would help them live with their problem. Furthermore, having been a member of faculties responsible for training psychology interns, it was clear to me that nothing anyone else was doing was working either. I felt the dissatisfaction, frustration, and stress of continually trying to help people find an answer that was as yet unknown to me and my profession. Thus, I began my search for something more substantial and practical.

I began by looking outside the boundaries of what I had been taught. Initially what I found was startling. It had never even crossed my mind that there existed more psychotherapies than those to which I had been exposed during my training. But as I was to find out, there was an immense number of psychotherapies—literally hundreds of them. I began immediately to "pan for gold," but what I found ranged from the silly, bizarre, painful, or harmful to what amounted to various combinations of psychotherapies with which I was already familiar. Most important of all was the fact that the results associated with these approaches were at best no better than what my own experience had revealed. What I found was so disillusioning that, after a few years of being in the field of psychology, I contemplated changing my profession.

In 1977, however, something happened that changed all this. What happened is something that I will probably spend the rest of my life hoping to understand, although the results have been very explicable. Quite simply, my understanding changed. As a result of this change, I began to see in a very clear and often amusing manner what I as a therapist was doing. In fact, I began to recognize all the ways in which we as psychotherapists, researchers, and teachers were unknowingly working against the very thing we were trying to find—mental health. In the course of a relatively short span of time, I began to realize the answer to the riddle that has eluded the field of mental health. I began to realize that the secret to reversing mental disorders that by today's beliefs are incurable, was to proceed in a direction opposite to most everything I had been doing to my patients. For the first time in my personal and professional life, I felt that I had found a solid psychological fact. As an experience this understanding was at a much deeper level than anything I had ever been led to believe possible during my professional training.

Since then, many people, especially psychologists and psychiatrists, have asked me what I was doing or what I did that changed me or caused me to come to these insights. The answer to this question is as tricky as it is essential to understand. The answer to this question is that it all began with "listening," although at the time I did not know what I was listening to. Allow me to explain. As part of my professional search, I was attending an eight-day program on different approaches to psychotherapy and counseling. Toward the end of the week I happened to attend an unscheduled evening talk given by theosopher Sydney Banks, author of *Second Chance*. Although to this day I cannot recollect the details of Mr. Banks's talk, what I heard was something so utterly simple and logical that it bordered on an insult to my intelligence—and yet, at the same time, was captivating. Up to that time listening had not been one of my strong points. In the course of my professional life, analyzing, interpreting, comparing, contrasting, and critiquing had become a way of life. On this occasion, however, I quite unexpectedly found myself "listening" and soon became enthralled by a barrage of excitingly fresh insights and ideas that I had never before envisioned. The most amazing thing about it was the fact that these new thoughts were coming from the very direction in which Mr. Banks had been pointing. They were coming from within my own consciousness. In any case, that evening something very definite changed in *my* understanding that changed my life. It was this shift in my understanding that continued to unfold over the coming years in the form of a set of insights that have come to be known as the Psychology of Mind. Although I could never hold Sydney Banks responsible for what I have subsequently realized, developed, and written about as a psychologist, I will be forever grateful to him for pointing me in the direction of my own gold-mine and for the wisdom that he has contributed to my profession, my science, and my world.

At the point in my career that I began to realize these insights leading to the development of the Psychology of Mind, I did not fully appreciate their profundity. At that time these insights seemed to be so simple and obvious that it was still unbelievable to me that they could even begin to bridge the immense gaps in our psychological knowledge or answer the multitude of incredibly complex questions that had been formulated in a century of psychological thinking. I had always assumed that if the answers to such questions were to be found they would be as complex as the questions. The opposite, of course, turned out to be true. Practicing psychology with the understanding that these simple insights brought allowed me to see people positively change to degrees unheard of in the mental-health field. The consistency of such results made it increasingly clear that these seemingly simple insights were only the visible peaks of a set of new psychological principles that in a short period of time would surface with the subtlety of a mountain range, providing psychology with a more clearly defined view of mental health.

In 1979 I was introduced to Dr. Roger Mills, who had been an administrator of a large community mental-health center, and had heard about my work. One year later Dr. Mills visited Miami and we put our ideas on paper, and thus began the Psychology of Mind.

Introduction

The manuscript was subsequently published by Med-Psych Publications in 1982 under the title *Sanity, Insanity, and Common Sense: The Missing Link in Understanding Mental Health.* By this time Dr. Mills had moved to Miami and had helped me to establish the Advanced Human Studies Institute in Coral Gables, Florida, as a center where this new psychology could continue to be developed, taught, and applied free from any restraints or limitations.

In the years that followed the opening of the Institute, hundreds of professionals from all over the United States came to Coral Gables to find out about this "new psychology." These professionals included psychologists, psychiatrists, physicians, nurses, social workers, educators, substance abuse counselors, administrators, and businesspeople. Soon formal and informal reports of their successes began to filter back to the Institute. This was the most precious fuel for our fire.

In 1986 *Sanity, Insanity, and Common Sense* was brought to the attention of Ballantine Books by a prominent Florida businessman who had acquired the publishing rights to the book in 1985 and who, in my opinion, genuinely recognized the deep implications of this new psychology. Without hesitation, Ballantine decided to republish the book. At this time I decided that a major revision was in order. So, with the added assistance of Darlene Stewart, a specialist in education and counseling psychology who had trained at the Institute several years earlier, the book was totally revised and updated.

One of the purposes of this book is to assist the reader to recognize and reconsider some ultimately important assumptions and beliefs upon which the traditional psychological theories and therapies are based. The importance of doing this lies in the fact that people in this society are presently at a point where they are increasingly looking toward the psychological realm for answers to the problems that they face in their day-to-day lives. It is almost impossible to find an institution that is not beginning to utilize psychology. Businesses, governments, churches, schools, prisons, hospitals, and police departments are all beginning to introduce the theories and techniques of psychology into their organizations. We are presently witnessing the "psychologizing" of society which is potentially both good news and bad news. The potentially good news is that there is a growing recognition that understanding how we as people work psychologically is central to the success or failure of *every* facet of human endeavor. This is certainly true. One need only view a television, listen to a radio, or read a newspaper to realize that the events we are witnessing represent the end product of our collective level of understanding and mental health. If a means, a psychology, were realized that would raise the level of understanding and mental health, it would mean that many of the problems that we are presently unsuccessfully struggling with in this society would begin to disappear. The potentially bad news is that if what is weaved into the fabric of a society is an inaccurate or otherwise misconceived psychology, the results could be devastating.

But perhaps the main purpose of this book is to give the reader a glimpse of some new and exciting observations that have begun to *totally* change the way in which mental-health professionals understand and treat psychological disturbances. For this reason, this book is filled to the brim with self-evident observations and statements representing a complete reversal of what theorists in psychology and psychiatry have carved in the granite of tradition. It is hoped that what is contained in this book will provide us, as a society, with a higher level of understanding. This new level of understanding will help us to break through to a healthier approach to helping people who have misplaced their sanity—similar to the way in which the field of medicine had to break through numerous beliefs in its evolution. For example, at one point the practice of indiscriminately bleeding people as a treatment for disease was considered acceptable by the medical profession. However, as the knowledge of what blood was emerged, it was realized how precious this substance was and that the haphazard use of this practice was not in the best interests of the patient's health. At first this newfound knowledge was resisted, not because the knowledge was complex but because bloodletting had been a standard medical practice. The idea of discontinuing the practice was considered heresy by physicians who truly believed bloodletting to be therapeutic. Yet it was insights such as this one, which came from outside the currently held frame of reference, that contributed to the development of the medical profession. Similarly, we will present some new principles of human psychological functioning that take us beyond the frame of reference of psychology today. While it is unavoidable that this will change what we as psychotherapists and counselors do, I would caution you not to look upon this volume primarily as an admonishment to abandon certain practices but rather as an encouragement to look upon them from a fresh perspective. In other words, it is the new knowledge, the new logic of how we as human beings function mentally, that is the important point. We have tried to express, as best as we can, the Psychology of Mind and its connection to mental health. You already possess common sense and wisdom. What we are offering is an answer which, when properly understood, will assist you in realizing that your consistent mental well-being is only one thought away.

EMS
Coral Gables, Florida

Sanity, Insanity,
and Common
Sense

CHAPTER ONE

The Nature
of a Science
and the Field
of Mental
Health

In 1973 a fascinating and revealing article entitled "On Being Sane in Insane Places," was published in the scientific journal *Science*. [1] This article was an account of the experiences of eight mentally healthy individuals, who, for the purposes of a scientific experiment, posed as individuals seeking psychiatric help. The group included psychologists, a psychiatrist, a pediatrician, a housewife, and a psychology graduate student. Each of the eight pseudopatients went to a different hospital and presented a generalized ambiguous complaint that lacked any substantiation or validity. On the basis of their general initial complaint, all of these healthy individuals were admitted to the hospital for psychiatric treatment. Other than falsifying their initial complaint, name, and occupation, each pseudopatient provided each hospital with truthful medical and social histories. Most important, aside from their initial complaint, the pseudopatients voiced no further problems nor did they exhibit any signs of psychological or emotional distress. In other words, they behaved in a perfectly normal fashion.

On twelve different hospital admissions (some of the eight pseudopatients went to more than one hospital), the pseudopatients were assessed to be psychotic; eleven were diagnosed as suffering from schizophrenia while one was diagnosed as manic-depressive. These mentally healthy people were kept in the hospital for periods that ranged from 7 to 52 days (the average stay was 19 days) and were prescribed varying combinations of psychiatric medications that included antidepressives and antipsychotics such as Elavil, Stelazine, Compazine, and Thorazine. During the course of their treatment, nearly 2,100 pills were administered to the pseudopatients (most of which were discarded, with only two pills actually taken). Upon discharge, all of the pseudopatients received a diagnosis of schizophrenia, "in remission."

During their lengthy hospitalizations, not one of the pseudo-patients was recognized by the staff of any of the twelve hospitals as being a normal, healthy person. Not one was suspected of having been misdiagnosed. In fact, quite the opposite was true. Once these people were labeled as psychotic, their behavior, which would have been considered healthy in another context, was consistently perceived as dysfunctional. The only people who noticed that something was amiss were other patients. One of the patients remarked, "You're not crazy. You're a journalist or a professor [referring to the pseudopatient's note-taking]. You're someone who is here to check up on the hospital." "It is clear," concludes the author of the article, "that we cannot distinguish the sane from the insane in psychiatric hospitals."

Studies like "On Being Sane in Insane Places" (of which there have been many variations) are often referred to as "anomalies." Anomalies are bothersome to any field because they are exceptions to the rule. In the sciences, anomalies have never been popular with the keepers and defenders of the established rules or theories. Why? Because anomalies highlight the inadequacies of established theories. Yet as one looks at the development of a science, it becomes increasingly obvious that these inconsistencies or irregularities are the harbingers of new knowledge, in that they prompt the scientist to look beyond the boundaries of established ways of thinking. Anomalies often raise questions that would otherwise not be entertained. For example, what are the costs to a society when its mental-health experts are not only unable to recognize or diagnose mental health, but are predisposed to perceive the sane as being insane? To what degree are our traditional treatment approaches unknowingly promoting insanity? To what degree are the problems of our society a direct or indirect result of our inability to see mental health when it is present? Or, on the other side of the question, we might wonder, given that we presently are not

6

expert at recognizing or understanding mental health, what are the potential benefits to society if we were to realize such mastery? In other words, what would happen if the field of psychology were to become a more exact science?

THE NATURE OF A SCIENCE

Over the last century, the field of psychology has debated whether psychotherapy is a science or an art form. This raises the question, what is it that makes a discipline a science? The commonality among the accepted sciences, such as mathematics, physics, chemistry, or engineering, is that each of these scientific disciplines has a consistent, uniform set of underlying principles which apply to all phenomena included within that field.

We have assumed that physics and chemistry are assured the status of a science by virtue of the fact that the phenomena studied in these fields are observable and measurable. Yet physics and chemistry, more often than not, deal with phenomena that are not directly observable to the senses. This is the case in atomic and molecular level phenomena and the actions of electromagnetic and gravitational fields. Yet the principles used to describe these phenomena are generally accepted as scientific.

Similarly, mathematics is also accepted as a science, although the phenomena studied in this field are even more abstract and intangible than they are in psychology. Mathematics has been accepted as a science because the principles upon which mathematical relationships are based are logically consistent and precise. Certain transformations and relationships are defined in terms of principles that, if properly understood and consistently used, will result in the correct answer. These relationships are defined by principles that are universal in that they apply equally to all problems that fall within that area of mathematics. This leads us to the conclusion that there must be more to making a discipline a science than the nature of the subject matter. So, what do the fields of physics, chemistry and mathematics have in common that is missing in the field of psychology? The answer is that psychology is lacking underlying, consistent, unifying principles that lead to predictable results.

THE STATUS OF PSYCHOLOGY

The field of psychology has not yet realized its scientific potential, not because of the nature of the object of study, but rather, because its level of understanding has not been sufficiently deep enough to see the big picture. Consequently, instead of relating diverse phenomena to a unifying framework of understanding, our traditional formulations break up or fragment the phenomena they are studying to such an overwhelming degree that they are confusing rather than clarifying. Psychology, to date, has a myriad of theories and models, many of which operate from a base of assumptions that are mutually inconsistent or even contradictory to one another. Yet each of these varying schools of thought gets support from its adherents within accepted academic and professional ranks. Psychologist Raymond Corsini[2] listed 240 different psychotherapies, which tells the tale of the state of the art in psychology.

The inconsistent framework which the field has accepted regarding human behavior has resulted in inconsistent observations and results. Patients going to different therapists will often be told completely different reasons for why they are experiencing problems and correspondingly, different treatments, all based on contradictory assumptions about the source of human behavior. The variation that exists between psychological theories is as great as the variation of factors those theories are trying to explain.

For example, *Science 86* recently focused on this very topic in an article entitled "Therapy Under Analysis."[3] In addition to highlighting the proliferation of psychotherapies (more than 250), as well as a growth trend in the number of people seeking help through psychological counseling (80 million people), this article included a particularly revealing section entitled "The Shrinking of George." George was the name of a fictitious character whose case history was presented to four different therapists practicing four different brands of therapy: behavioral therapy, family therapy, psychodynamic therapy, and cognitive therapy. The psychotherapists reviewed George's predicament and offered their views on how they would help this man in treatment.

Briefly, George is a 31-year-old man who has been married for five years. George recalls his childhood as a happy one and described his parents as being "loving and fair" toward him and his older sister. He remembered his mother as a quiet and passive woman whose main disciplinary tactic was a doleful look. His father, an engineer, was very protective of his wife and when correcting his children often remarked, "This is really going to disappoint your mother." George stated that there was no history of any psychological disorders in his family. The problem, as presented in this article, involved a pretty and flirtatious new typist, Laura, who had begun working for George, an administrator in a state government office that manages small business development. George initially found Laura's seductiveness amusing and in fact planned to tell his wife, Ann, about it one evening. Before he could do so, however, he and Ann had a fight over who would be using the car that evening. In his anger, George ended up not telling Ann about Laura and at the time even felt a moment of satisfaction in keeping this information to himself. In the subsequent weeks, Laura made it clear to George that she wanted to have an affair with him. George, however, did not comply. Sometime later, George, who has played the bassoon since he was in the fourth grade, played a noontime concert at the park as part of a quintet. Ann and Laura both showed up (separately) to watch George perform, and when George saw them he suddenly began to feel humiliated by what he thought were his "artistic pretentions," the ungainliness of his bassoon, and the amateurish nature of his group. From this point on, George began to avoid practicing playing his bassoon and even dropped out of the musical groups to which he belonged. George began to experience anxiety, and one night he awakened at 4 A.M. and resolved to get his life in order. The next day he suggested to his wife that they have a baby (Ann conceived three weeks later) and asked a co-worker to complain about Laura's performance (Laura was reassigned to another office). In spite of all of these changes, George was very unhappy. He became afraid that Laura would find out why she was transferred and he actively avoided running into her at work. When he did run into Laura, George was surprised that she still acted seductively toward him, though now he imagined that she was mocking him. One night, while making love to his wife, George fantasized he was with Laura and subsequently, this fantasy persisted. George began to experience insomnia and anxiety and became increasingly irritated in response to what he called Ann's "sickliness" (the nausea Ann experienced during the first part of her pregnancy). George sought psychological help three weeks after his fantasies of Laura began. His reason for seeking help was to find the "self-discipline" necessary to be a good husband, father, and musician. George voiced that he did not want to to see his child as an intrusion in his life and wished to be able to sleep through the night.

Briefly, here is what each of the four psychotherapists saw as being the cause of George's problem and what they would do to help him resolve it.

The behavioral therapist began this way: "What I would first try to do is 'operationalize' George's complaints—get him to define them as specifically as possible. . . . Once we had defined behaviors he would like to change, I would have him monitor what he's doing that's a problem. . . . In George's case, probably the easiest behavior to monitor would be sleep—what time he wakes up, and either how many times he wakes up in the middle of the night or how long those times were. . . . Once the problem behaviors had been pinned down . . . I'd teach him a relaxation technique. . . ." This therapist goes on to note that once George had learned the relaxation technique and could relax she would ". . . have him think about being in bed and having sex with Ann . . . if he starts thinking about Laura, he could signal me—by closing his eyes tighter, or moving his elbow—and I'd say, 'Stop, think about Ann.'" This therapist also suggested that she could help George out of his anxiety about Laura by using a role reversal technique in which George would make believe he was Laura and the psychotherapist would make believe she was George. In this way George would be able to interact with Laura. George could even use Laura as a fulcrum for lifting his musical inclinations out of the doldrums by using another technique whereby "every time he talks to her [Laura], he could reward himself by putting aside $5 toward a new bassoon. . . ." In the same vein, ". . . if he [George] was supposed to do his relaxation five nights a week and he only did it three, he would have to write a $5 check to, say, the National Rifle Association every time he missed." This therapist recommended four months of intensive therapy, followed by less intensive therapy several times a month.

The family therapist saw George's predicament in a different way. The family therapist would spend only 10 or 15 minutes talking about the presenting symptoms. Then the therapist would get a history of the relationship between him [George] and his wife, going back to when they first met, and how the relationship developed, what the big events in it were, and how they each reacted to those events. The other thing the therapist would try to do is to get a more detailed picture of George's extended family. This therapist would sketch a three–generational family tree of both George and Ann's family, where each family member would be described in terms of their character traits, accomplishments, responsibilities, emotional, social and physical impairments, age at death, and cause of death. This chart is tacked to the wall during therapy and the family therapist notes that ". . . I always keep that in the background—always a context for what's happening here and now." As this therapist sees it, "George's interest in another woman . . . could very well be a reaction to some emotional preoccupation of his wife's that he perceives . . . if you took a history of what's going on in his wife's family right now you might find that her mother was just diagnosed with a serious disease like breast cancer. . . ." This therapist goes on to suggest that "one of the things George needs to do eventually is develop a closer, more emotionally substantial relationship with his mother's siblings, and through that, continue to learn about this person, who was his mother. . . . The same is true for his father and his father's family. This is one of the best ways for him [George] to find out who he is and how he got to be who he is." This therapist suggests George be in therapy for a year or two.

The psychodynamic therapist presents still another view of George's reality. This therapist is ". . . struck by the kind of work George does . . . he manages other people's development, but he's having some problem managing his own. . . . He says his parents were 'loving and fair.' Well 'fair' isn't a word a person normally uses to describe his parents, unless fairness was some kind of issue. It may be that all the normal sibling rivalry got buried by the mother. . . . It sounded to me like the mother ran the home. . . . And that makes me think of George having as a model a father who . . . hides behind his wife's skirts. . . . George is in so many ways such a little guy—not sure of himself as a man, not feeling like a substantial, solid person . . . and here he is, playing the bassoon, one of the largest instruments in the orchestra, as if it's something for him to compensate with. And his wife's pregnancy and sickness seem to be contributing to a further deterioration of his sense of manliness, so he decides to compensate by getting a bigger and better bassoon. This is getting me to think about the baby representing some further injury to his sense of masculinity. That's unusual—becoming a father usually helps men feel more phallically potent . . . in George's case, it's more as if Ann's growing and he's shrinking. . . . And now he becomes obsessed with Laura. Usually obsessions are a way of controlling aggression. You wonder how much anger toward his wife about the pregnancy is tied up in that. And men can experience intercourse with a pregnant wife as an attack on the baby . . . so maybe the obsessive thoughts about Laura are some way of blocking out that aggression. . . ." This therapist foresees four or five sessions a week of analysis for George, probably for several years.

The cognitive therapist, on the other hand, would treat George by having George recount the bad experiences of the previous week. From this data, the therapist would jot down the critical events as well as the accompanying thoughts and feelings. In between sessions, George would be asked to keep track of his responses by writing them down in a journal during or as soon as possible following an emotional upset. The therapy according to this therapist, "would then consist of disputing these thoughts." The once-a-week sessions should last about six months.

The above four examples of psychotherapy constitute the mainstream of traditional psychological approaches to helping people. And this is why if one considers that, according to this article, there are at least 246 other forms of therapy being practiced, each one being as different from the next as different can be, along with the fact that 80 million people are trying to find their sanity through such counseling, it is not difficult to imagine why sanity appears to be an elusive commodity.

The end product of this confusion is that psychotherapy is still characterized by inconclusive and uncertain results.

SPECIALIZATION IN PSYCHOLOGY

In spite of inconsistent therapeutic results, after one century of development, the field continues to lean toward further diversification and specialization. Some psychologists suggest that we need to develop specific techniques to accomplish specific kinds of behavior change with specific types of patients, applied by specific types of therapists. It has been suggested that to accomplish such a feat one would need (1) a classification system for clients, (2) a classification system for problems, (3) a classification system of therapeutic approaches, and (4) a classification system for therapists. Rather than looking for a common denominator that would collapse the variation into an understandable pattern, the traditional direction of psychology has been to deal with the variation itself.

Specialization within the field is a further example of variation. In the field of psychology today, we have specialists for eating disorders, aging problems, substance abuse, marital discord, incest, child abuse, sexual dysfunction, psychosomatic complaints, phobias, anxiety, depression, stress, and on and on. There are literally hundreds of specialities in the field. Yet it is common to have a client who crosses specialties. For example, people who abuse alcohol are frequently the same people who have a disordered family life, poor work performance, relationship problems, sexual dysfunction, and low self-esteem. Which speciality should claim this client?

SPECIALIZATION AND SCIENTIFIC ADVANCEMENT

In the early days of physics, scientists studied manifested phenomena separately. Why did this practice occur? Because all of the phenomena appeared to be different and separate from each other. Thus some early physicists were specialists in heat, some in electricity, some in gravity, some in optics, others in mechanics, and so on. However, at a certain stage in the field's development, people began to see some interesting connections. For example, the physicist recognized that heat could be turned into electricity, which, in turn, could be turned into light or mechanical energy, or could generate magnetic forces. Furthermore, these processes could even be reversed. Once physicists began to recognize the universal principle of energy, this understanding clarified that similarities were more important than differences in finding out how the physical universe worked. Different specialties and categories were collapsed and the differences became less and less important. The principles of Einstein's theory of general relativity showed clearly and convincingly that all energy and substance could be broken down to the same basic phenomena which undergo transformations from one form to another in very predictable and understandable ways.

Similar to the early years in physics, traditional psychology was constructed at the level of observing and explaining the external differences. The field has become fragmented and specialized by focusing on the details of people's problems. By doing this, we have divided and segmented our study of human behavior into literally hundreds of isolated theories and practices. The end result of this practice is lack of theoretical consistency as well as the lack of therapeutic results. So whether psychotherapy is considered a science or an artform, it is still in the same boat as described by Jerome Frank of Johns Hopkins University, who wrote: "At this point it must be emphasized that the failure to find differences in improvement rate from different forms or amounts of psychotherapy is a sign of ignorance, not knowledge. . . ."[4]

The field's inability to recognize its predicament has prompted professionals to focus on this topic at length. For example, in discussing the scientific level of our present framework of psychological approaches, psychologists Ivan London and Warren Thorngate noted:

But for the social sciences, where are the promised successes? Despite all his [the social scientist's] efforts and firm faith in an ultimate payoff, these successes are still to be exhibited. The radical reorientations that initiated the great advances of physics (relativity and quantum theory) have no counterpart in the social sciences. Instead, the social sciences continue to be bound futilely to the orientations of classical physics, from which they have elaborated naive conceptions of force, energy, least action, equilibrium, etc., seeming to promise much but accomplishing little. The fault may be in what we are trying to do. The model for progress we have been emulating may have misdirected us and dissipated our energies not because it was wrong, but precisely because it has been wedded to classical orientations . . . yet even in physics, classical orientations have been replaced, while in the social sciences they tenaciously persist in spite of their record of failure and skepticism of the few mavericks in the field.[5]

THE LIMITATIONS OF THE TRADITIONAL MODELS

The inconsistencies in our present psychological theories and the inconsistent results that follow make it clear that the field needs a new, more unified direction. Psychology will not derive more universal, more accurate principles of human psychological functioning from reexamining or recycling the currently accepted frequently oppositional theories. Rather, we must begin to look at our observations, our data, and our experience from a new perspective, one that is outside of and free from the biases or limitations of currently accepted models. In the same vein, Albert Einstein and Leopold Infeld noted: "Successful revolt against the accepted view results in unexpected and completely different developments, becoming a source of new philosophical aspects."[6]

PSYCHOLOGICAL COMMON DENOMINATORS: A NEW DIRECTION FOR THE FIELD

The field of psychology has lacked a logically consistent, universally applicable set of fundamental principles of human functioning that hold their predictive power across all variations of human behavior. What has been missing in psychology that would provide the next evolutionary step has been unifying general principles which would bring what we already know into clear focus and provide a greater understanding of human psychological functions. Unifying principles would provide the field of psychology with a new direction, a direction which points toward the integration

17

rather than the diversification of knowledge. Professionals often forget that the purpose of scientific research and discovery, as Einstein and Infeld put it, is to "reduce the apparent complexity of natural phenomena to some simple, fundamental ideas and relations . . . to discover some essential, common features hidden beneath the surface of some external differences, to form on this basis a new successful theory."[7]

Psychotherapy is precisely the arena where people seek to "reduce the apparent complexity" of their experience of life. However, as we noted in the introduction, the traditional psychotherapeutic approaches that Roger, Darlene, and I were initially trained in, seemed to complicate matters by introducing even more worrisome thoughts into people's lives.

As we began to recognize the fallacy of trying to work at the level of differences, we turned our attention to recognizing the fundamental ideas or the principles that underlied all the differences. We wanted to uncover the essential, common features that existed for the field of psychology. We were looking for a way to understand the complete range of human psychological experience which included not only problems, but also states of happiness or mental health. We felt that a truly scientific psychology of human behavior should be based on principles that held consistently across the entire range of human experience, and that included the experience of mental health as well as that of mental illness.

The principles of human psychological functioning that emerged as a result of that search have come to be known as the principles of Psychology of Mind.

CHAPTER TWO

The Principles of Psychology of Mind: The Principle of Thought and Reality

When some degree of factual understanding about any phenomenon is realized, principles emerge that embody this new and deeper levels of understanding. Such a principle cannot point toward contradiction. This is illustrated in the case of mathematics, where there exist principles which guide the mathematician toward an obvious solution or a recognizable contradictory answer that leaves no doubt regarding its falsity. When a mathematical problem cannot be resolved, it is because we have misunderstood the principle or have made an error in computation. In either case, the principle itself remains accurate.

When this is understood, it becomes obvious why psychological principles are not amenable to personal use, in the sense that they could be used on people, or by people in a manipulative way. Instead, like the principles of mathematics, they impersonally describe a function and the impact of that function on a system of experiential variables.

From the previous discussion, it is clear that the majority of traditional concepts in the field of psychology do not qualify as principles for the simple reason that they apply only to specific cases under a host of qualifications. Such concepts do not lead to answers. In fact, when applied to the general population, such concepts raise more questions and lengthen the list of probable answers about human behavior. Because of the lack of bona fide principles, traditional psychological interventions often point in the direction of complexity rather than simplicity, fragmentation rather than unification. This lack of unifying principles indicates that psychology has relied on concepts, which are not the principle, but the *effect* of principle.

During the course of our professional work, we have recognized a set of four principles of human psychological functioning that

21

underlie our experiences and behaviors as human beings. Psychological principles describe the functional relationship between thoughts, experiences, and behavior. The results of this relationship are precise and constant, irrespective of the details of personality, life situation, or past history. Consequently these principles provide simple, common-sense understanding of mental illness, emotional disturbance, stress, and addictive or compulsive behaviors, and also shed light on how to reverse the process that leads to these disorders in order to eliminate illness and establish mental health. There is no doubt that the principles of human psychological functioning that we will present in this book represent a new direction for the field of mental health. As you will note, this set of principles is related to four common denominators or constants that are common to all human beings. These four constants, the basis of what we call the Psychology of Mind, are

1. The capability of each human being to formulate thought and the thought system that each human being has created.

2. The separate reality of individual differences that every unique thought system creates.

3. The capability of human beings to understand the nature of their own psychological functioning.

4. Feelings and emotions as indicators of the quality and direction of human psychological functioning.

The principles derived from these constants alter the frame of reference of how we think about mental illness and mental health. These principles point the field of psychology in a direction that is beyond the field's present base of assumptions and theories. Furthermore, an understanding of these principles alters the frame of reference from which we derive our approaches to treating all forms of human psychological malfunctioning. In addition to giving us a fresh perspective on the subject of mental illness as well as mental health, these principles shed new perspective on the source of perception, feeling, and behavior. In this chapter, we will introduce the first two principles of human functioning.

PRINCIPLE 1: THE CENTRAL ROLE OF THOUGHT IN FORMING EVERYDAY PSYCHOLOGICAL EXPERIENCE

Perhaps the most important fact of human functioning is that human beings have the capacity to think and what a person thinks has the power to shape personal reality. "As a man thinks, so it shall be" is a very profound statement of fact because thought is the link between a human being and the reality in which that human being lives. Thought is the dimension that determines the quality of our experience at any moment in time. However, we are so closely identified with the contents of our thoughts that we rarely step back to realize that our beliefs, values, theories, and assumptions are an effect of the fact that we are thinking. We rarely realize that we are using our ability to think to create specific thought content.

A psychological common denominator, or principle, cannot exist at the level of thought content because no two people have the same thought content. The content of thinking is the variable. In order to find the common denominator or the principle, we must bypass the variation in what is thought about and go to the deeper, more fundamental level of human functioning, which is the human being's *ability* to think. It is the ability to think that underlies all the content of what is thought about. This ability to think enables an individual to create an infinite variety of content. The ability to think is the constant factor which does not vary from individual to individual. It is the constant from which all variation in thought is produced. The capacity to understand this fact exists at the level of recognizing a psychological principle.

The Thought System

As each of us has moved through our experiences in life, we have used our abiltiy to think to develop and store a personal thought system. This system of thought is a sophisticated, inter-woven network of habitual thought patterns, including concepts, judgments, attitudes, opinions, assumptions, beliefs, and expec-tations. We use this system of thought to compare, examine, theo-rize, generalize, measure, and remember. All of these are the basis for interpreting our experience in the present from the perspective of our experience in the past. (Our past experiences exist in the present, in the form of thoughts.) These stored or habitual thoughts are the thoughts that we use as a basis for interpreting the significance of present events in our lives. Every thought, idea, bias, or concept within this system of thought is stored as memory, in very much the same way as a computer stores bits of data.

A thought system exists as a bundle of associaitons stored in the brain. There is no longer any doubt that the brain is a biological computer capable of projecting thought as a sensory-motor expe-rience. Using the analogy of the computer, the brain can be viewed as the "hardware" of the computer and the thought system as the program, or the "software."

Thoughts, based on stored information, help us navigate through daily life. For example, we are able to store away our language, our address or our telephone number and can call them up at will when we need them. Because they are stored in our biological computer, we don't have to relearn them every day.

Every personal thought system is a sophisticated, interwoven network of thoughts. Thoughts central to a certain theme are called beliefs. In every thought system, there is a unique interdependence and logical connection among the thoughts or beliefs within that system. For example, if a person believes that someone of another race cannot be trusted, the person with that belief will have rational reasons to support it. This belief will result in certain perceptions and behaviors which, in turn, will elicit a particular response from people of another race. We perceive situations in a way that conforms with and validates our system of thinking. In turn, the perceptions and experiences that emerge from a particular way of thinking appear to support what we think. Thus the belief will be validated in the external situation. A woman who believes that men cannot be trusted is a woman who will never experience a man that she can trust. The experiences that come out of our separate realities are real to us regardless of how nonexistent they may be to others, or how nonexistent they are in fact.

There is a direct connection between personal beliefs and personal experience of life. A thought system is a perceptual filter through which people screen and interpret all incoming data. When we function psychologically via our thought system, perception is based on interpretation. In other words, the content of thought becomes the perceptual filter through which we screen events, situations, and people to create our moment-to-moment personal reality. Because we have a thought system, to one degree or another we all unconsciously interpret our experience to mean what it has meant to us in the past. Because of our thought system, we continually contaminate the present with our memories of the past.

Unaware of this screening and interpreting process, we innocently believe that our thinking tells us the truth. We trust that the world really exists as we personally interpret it, so in essence, we let our conditioned and unconscious screening dictate subsequent thinking. For example, because of his past experience, John may assume that when his wife, Ann, is quiet, she is blaming him for doing something wrong. Locked into this interpretation, John will feel guilty whenever Ann is quiet. This guilt will predispose John to certain persistent behaviors that will inevitably end up with Ann mad at him. At which point John will validate his interpretation by saying, "I knew you were quiet because you were mad at me."

Each human being has the capacity to take a thought-created world and bring it to life. Thought produces a reality that becomes our experience. We have thoughts about people, objects, and events. It is our thought that we actually know, although we have assumed all our lives that we knew the thing itself. We believe that we have authentic contact with the world, when in fact what we have contact with is our thought about the world. Our thought represents something that exists separate and apart from our thinking about it.

We assume that our thoughts are fairly reliable descriptions of the thing they represent, but this is not always the case as was so brilliantly illustrated in "On Being Sane in Insane Places." What was more interesting was how easily the misperception of reality illustrated in this experiment could be reshaped into an opposite misperception. A follow-up experiment was carried out among the staff of a research and teaching hospital, who doubted that such errors could occur at their hospital. To test this possibility, the psychiatric staff was informed that during the following three months, one or more pseudopatients would try to gain admission to their hospital. All staff members, psychiatrists, physicians, psychologists, nurses, and attendants were asked to rate each patient at admission or on the ward in terms of the likelihood that he or she was a pseudopatient. The results of this study were very interesting. Out of a total of 193 patients admitted for psychiatric treatment, 41 were judged with a high degree of confidence to be pseudopatients by at least one staff member. Twenty-three patients were suspected of being pseudopatients by at least one psychiatrist and 19 patients were suspected of being pseudopatients by one psychiatrist and one staff member. What is so interesting about these results? The experimenters never sent anyone to this hospital! The only thing that was sent was a thought (an expectation) and the pseudopatients "appeared."

A thought system will maintain its own internal consistency. This characteristic of a thought system exists to the point that the acceptance of a new idea is limited to, and affected by, the existing content. A system of thought will reshape the new idea to conform to the context of what is already accepted. If this new idea is not compatible to the existing beliefs, that new idea will be attacked or disregarded. Like most other systems, a thought system maintains its integrity and will only allow change according to specific parameters that are dictated by the existing structure. Once a certain set of beliefs has been defined as the system, new data put into that system will change, following the rules that have already been set by the existing structure. Any thought that is plugged into this existing set will automatically follow the rules of the existing interpretations and biases.

A Mathematical Analogy

The mathematical analogy to the psychological phenomenon of a thought system is called a function. In mathematical science, a function is a framework within which we define a certain set of rules or laws of transformation. Once these rules have been defined, variables that are put into that function will be transformed, following the rules that have been defined for that function.

For example, the U.S. tax code is really a mathematical function that defines how much an individual must pay according to income, source of income, dependents, and applicable deductions. At the end of the year, each individual inputs his or her unique combination of figures, and the mathematical function underlying the present tax structure transforms those figures into the amount of tax due for the year. As is the case with any such function, a change in the reality of the outcome (the amount of tax to be paid) could occur either because the input figures changed, as would be the case if the individual's income increased or decreased, or if there were a change in the tax law (the rules of trans- formation).

Psychologically, each individual collects and combines learned attitudes, ideas, values, prejudices, and concepts into an accu- mulation of beliefs, combined in a way that is unique to that individual. Any event or situation in that person's experience is plugged into this existing thought system, and then that event will automatically be transformed and perceived in a manner dictated by the rules of the existing interpretations and biases. By using thought as a perceptual filter, we transform any experience into what we think it to be.

A system of thinking can be understood as setting up a field of reality. A "field" as used in physics means a configuration of forces acting in a particular area of space, such as the space around a magnet or between two electrically charged plates. Our thought system acts in a manner analogous to these fields in the sense that any stimulus that comes into an individual's field of reality is dis- torted, affected, or interpreted by the nature of the thoughts (e.g., beliefs, values, expectations, biases) that subsume his particular reality.

In a manner analogous to magnetic and other physical fields, if we turn off the current or otherwise remove the field, the distortion of forces acting on external stimuli no longer exists. The nature of the particular configuration of forces, when they are removed, is no longer a factor.

Thus the key to changing our own field of thinking is to discover the process by which this system gets activated and maintained in ourselves. The key to the solution is to realize that thinking is a *voluntary* function. Thinking is something that we do. Regardless of how it may appear, thoughts have no life of their own, separate and apart from the thinker. To understand this, we must make the distinction between the content of thinking and the capability to think. In other words, we must begin to recognize the function of thought.

Thought as a Function

As we have said before, a psychological common denominator, or principle, cannot exist at the level of thought content because every person's thought content differs from every other one. Instead of looking at the content, the variable, we look at the constant, which is the human being's ability to generate thought. The *ability* to think is the common denominator because that is what gives a human being the power to formulate content or details. The ability to think underlies all the specifics of what is thought about.

Most of us have lived our lives unconsciously wrapped up in the contents of our own thoughts, operating within the confines of our beliefs, attitudes, opinions, fears, and judgments and associated perceptions without realizing that it was we ourselves who created these thoughts in the first place. The moment we realize that our reality is a self-created world of thought, we begin to get a glimpse of the power that we have to change realities. A thinking human being holds the ultimate power to continue, drop, or suspend a pattern of negative thoughts that is holding together a negative reality.

Thought, Perception, Feelings, and Behavior

As we are beginning to see, there is a direct connection between a person's thought and that person's experience in life. In fact, the existence of thought systems is revealed by the perceptions, feelings, and behaviors that result from it. When human beings do not recognize the voluntary nature of their ability to selectively utilize their thought system, they have no choice but to unconsciously function within the limits of their thought systems. Unconsciously living within the limits of a thought system means that the individual will perceive life in the form dictated by the content of his or her past without ever realizing what is behind his or her experience in the present. This is in contrast to when the individual is conscious of what a thought system is and can more appropriately utilize the information within it as he or she deems necessary. In any case, *an activated thought system will determine exactly what an individual is experiencing at any given moment.*

Figure 1 illustrates how the function of thought, when unrecognized, activates stored thinking habits which determine perception and feeling, and culminates in behavior that is consistent with those perceptions and feelings. One thing that we start to see from this broader perspective is that perceptions, feelings, and behaviors have their source in thought. This is completely opposite to what most of us have been led to believe. What we can begin to see from this diagram is that everything that we observe through the filters of our thought system is already an interpretation. Once we accept this interpretation, we become locked into certain emotional and behavioral responses.

In the field of psychology we attempt to understand the sources

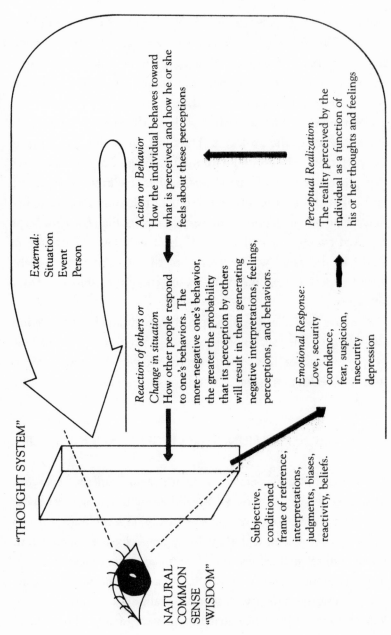

The reality perceived by the individual as a function of his or her thoughts and feelings

Perceptual Realization

Action or Behavior
How the individual behaves toward what is perceived and how he or she feels about these perceptions

Emotional Response:
Love, security confidence, fear, suspicion, insecurity depression

Reaction of others or Change in situation
How other people respond to one's behaviors. The more negative one's behavior, the greater the probability that its perception by others will result in them generating negative interpretations, feelings, perceptions, and behaviors.

External:
Situation
Event
Person

Subjective, conditioned frame of reference, interpretations, judgments, biases, reactivity, beliefs.

"THOUGHT SYSTEM"

NATURAL COMMON SENSE "WISDOM"

Figure 1

31

feelings or reactions by examining the details of the external situation. This practice has not and will not succeed. Attempting to find the source of feelings by searching through the details of the external circumstances is analogous to analyzing the picture on the movie screen in order to find the source of the picture. True understanding occurs only when we leave the picture and discover the existence of the projector. The function of thought exists as the projector of the content of thinking. Figure 2 further illustrates this process. As this figure shows, beliefs, feelings, perceptions, and behaviors are actually the results of thinking. Analyzing beliefs, feelings, perceptions, or behaviors is actually several steps removed from the actual source of these symptoms. This process works in the same way regardless of the content of a thought system, specific personality traits, or the circumstances of our situation.

We have looked at the principle of thought and have alluded to the fact that this psychological ability is what gives form to how people experience life. Another principle which follows directly from this realization is the principle of separate realities.

PRINCIPLE 2: THE PRINCIPLE OF SEPARATE REALITIES

The content of each person's thought system is unique because it is based on his or her personal stored interpretation of experiences in the past. Because of this, it is virtually impossible for any two people to have identical thought systems. Except for apparent broad cultural similarities, there are no consistent commonalities in the content of people's thought. Because of this fact, everyone lives in a separate reality. A separate reality is a personal psychological frame of reference that becomes the source of individual perceptions of reality.

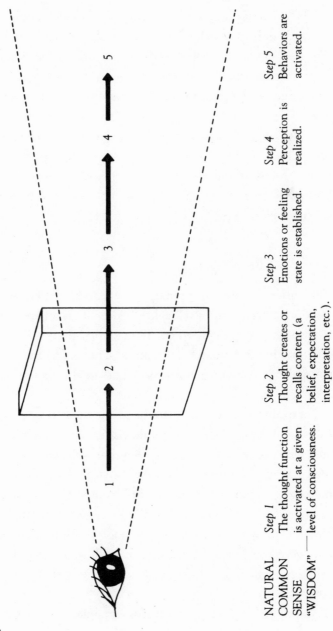

Figure 2

Sanity, Insanity, and Common Sense

The existence of separate realities has profound implications for the study of human behavior because it shows that *each person sees things differently*. Even within the same family or culture system, a wide variance in beliefs, concepts, and values are present. This is a fact that most people overlook because our thinking tells us that what we personally perceive is not only accurate, it is absolute. Our thinking tells us that the reality that we are perceiving is the only reality that exists. In order to see another person's separate reality, we must realize that ours is only one view of many possibilities. With this realization we are able to see with objectivity, other people's realities.

Levels of a Reality

In order to grasp this principle, the reader must begin to understand what we mean by a "reality." A reality is an apparency. It is how something *appears* to be. In actuality, there are many levels of reality implicit in any observation. This is why the reason for a particular perception cannot be found in the details of what is observed.

For example, when we go to the movie theater, we go expecting to see a film that depicts someone else's reality. Once in the theater, we sit back and look at a screen that is showing people speaking, moving, and interacting. As the story develops, we become increasingly absorbed in that reality. So much so, in fact, that we begin to feel the emotions that fit with the story. But once the movie is over, the lights come on and we are in a larger reality, one which includes the theater, as well as the fact that we are watching a film. In other words, a deeper reality has been uncovered.

To go one step further with this example, we can say that the movie is real only by appearance. What we have experienced as reality during the film existed because a film projector flashed a rapid series of still pictures on a screen. Since our eyes and brains could not keep up with the speed with which each picture was flashed on and off on the screen, the movie appeared as one continuous set of scenes which changed with respect to the movement of the characters and scenery. Whatever we perceive in life, whether it is a movie or our family or our job, it is real only because it appears so by virtue of our perspective at the moment.

A simple, elegant answer to understanding the riddle of individual differences exists when we see how individual thought systems work to create personal reality. With this realization, we are able to look beyond our own frame of reference to see our own biases and prejudices for what they are. We begin to see the content of our own thinking as a product of our conditioning, and so we begin to take our negative thoughts less seriously. We no longer attach our self-esteem to whether or not another person accepts our thoughts. As this happens, we are less reactive, less defensive, less tied to our personal view of things. We can use our "common sense" to see how all people function psychologically in this same way. This understanding allows us to feel secure in the face of another person's reality, or another culture's frame of reference. People begin to see their interactions with others as a predictable result of the interactions between separate thought systems.

The solution to any problem is to realize that the perception of the problem is a function of our ability to think in conjunction with the level of conscious understanding that thinking is taking place. Our thoughts formulate the reality that we experience moment to moment. In order to change our view of things (or help someone else to see how to change), we must get out of the frame of reference that is producing and maintaining that particular reality. Psychologically, if we attempt to work with the effects of our thought system, in the absence of realizing that we are thinking those effects into existence, we are missing the point. In other words, without our participation those effects are neutralized. Not realizing that we are the one who is doing the thinking, we give our power to our view of reality and then live in the world of its effects.

Take, for example, the case of Joy, a 40-year-old woman with a 25-year history of alcohol abuse. Joy comes from a home where both parents were heavy drinkers. Joy's parents were both successful professionals; however, their relationship and family life was an unhappy one. Although Joy harbored a great deal of resentment toward her parents because of their drinking, she began drinking in 10th grade, mostly out of an insecure feeling of wanting to fit in with her peer group. After graduating and marrying, Joy's drinking became her daily prescription for the unhappiness and stress that she was experiencing in her life. Before Joy was 27 years old she had two children and two divorces. Joy sought treatment for her drinking and very soon accepted the belief that she was an "alcoholic," in the absolute sense of the word. Within Joy's way of thinking, this meant that there was something in her genetic makeup that determined that for the rest of her life she would have to struggle against the desire to drink. Consequently, Joy's view of herself as a human being was built on a foundation of thoughts about herself as an alcoholic. She perceived herself to be at the mercy of a disease that had made her a bad wife and mother. She often cried at the thought that she had passed her disease on to her children. She worried whether she would be strong enough to say no if someone offered her a drink at a party. She wondered whether a new boyfriend would understand her when she announced to him that she "was an alcoholic." These thoughts along with the self-image they created, added more unhappiness to an already unhappy life.

The irony in Joy's case was that even when she had no desire to drink, and had not had a drink in two years, she still lived with the fear that the urge would catch her off guard and her life would once again be at the mercy of alcohol. Up to this point in her life, Joy was not aware of the fact that she was letting her thoughts shape her view of herself and her life. Eventually, Joy's outlook manifested itself in the breakup of her present relationship and she began drinking again. It was at this point that she was seen by one of the authors for treatment. As is the case with many people who have managed to stop drinking without any appreciable understanding of the psychological causes of substance abuse and dependence, Joy commented to her therapist that although she had been "abstinent," she had not been happy.

Joy's first surprise in therapy came when her therapist pointed out to her that her primary problem was not alcohol, but unhappiness. At first, this suggestion was totally unacceptable to Joy, who had always thought of her unhappiness as being caused by alcohol. As therapy progressed and Joy began to understand how thought shapes perceptions and feelings, it soon became obvious to her that she was trying to do the impossible: She was trying to keep alcohol from ruining the life of an "alcoholic," someone who will experience a lifelong craving or need for alcohol.

Joy finally came to the realization that it would be futile to try to change her life within the boundaries of her old thoughts, perceptions, and feelings of herself. This simple realization opened her eyes. For the first time in her life Joy understood that both her unhappiness and her attempts to blur it through drinking, had been coming from the same bundle of misperceptions—her thought system.

It did not take Joy long, following this realization, to realize that her alcoholism had been an effect of not knowing what she was doing in life. Her chronic unhappiness was the cause of her alcoholism. Once she became more stable and happy, she ceased to even think of alcohol as an issue in her life. In fact, one day, three years after having terminated therapy, Joy was at a party and was handed what she thought was a "virgin" fruit juice cocktail— it wasn't. Without giving it a second thought, Joy began to drink it. Her first thought was that there was something wrong with the drink because it did not taste right. Suddenly, the realization came that it was alcohol and that *she* did not like it. Joy called her therapist the very next morning, and thanked him for helping her find a new life.

Most of us, as individuals and professionals, have unknowingly lived our lives wrapped up in the contents of our own thoughts, operating within the details of our beliefs, theories, opinions, fears, and judgments. We have lived in this world of thought without realizing that we are the ones who have accepted and continue to give life to these thoughts in the first place. The moment that we realize that we are living in a world of thought that is our own creation, we are on the road to easier, more satisfying lives.

When we let go of the level of thinking that our particular thought system is absolute and we begin to see that reality is a relative thing, we begin to operate on a higher level of understanding. We find a way out of the limited field of personal thought. In order to do this we must first recognize and understand that there are psychological conditions in which we tend to lock ourselves in a separate reality of our own stored thought patterns. This leads us to the psychological principle of levels of consciousness.

CHAPTER THREE

Levels of Consciousness and Emotions

We've already described the first two principles of the Psychology of Mind, which are the principles of thought and separate realities. Principle 3 describes how a person's conscious knowledge of his or her psychological functioning affects personal reality. Principle 4 describes the role of feelings as indicators of the quality and direction of psychological functioning.

PRINCIPLE 3: LEVELS OF CONSCIOUSNESS

One of the observations that evolved into a fundamental principle of Psychology of Mind was that people, in the course of their day, moved in and out of more or less rational states of mind. Hospitalized psychiatric patients were at times caught up in their fantasies and irrational thoughts, but at other times, were not producing these thoughts, and functioned in a more objective or rational way. Observations of all kinds of people in everyday life confirmed that everyone goes in and out of different mood levels, and that the quality of our perceptions changes as our state of mind changes. In addition, in more rational states of mind, people are able to recognize that the way they were seeing things in lower moods was distorted in a negative direction (e.g., they had over-reacted, or thought that things were worse than they really were). We also observed that these mood changes were not linked to external changes in any systematic way, but rather fundamentally altered the way that the person perceived the significance of external events. As we shall explore in this chapter, we soon realized that each mood level actually constituted a different reality.

In all of the philosophies of the world, the concept of "levels of consciousness" is prominent. In the context of our realizations

41

about human psychology, we see that a level of consciousness actually refers to a principle of psychological functioning.

Within the present discussion, a level of consciousness is the degree to which a human being is aware that he or she is using an ability to think to formulate experience in life. The extent to which a person is conscious of his or her ability to utilize the function of thought, is the extent to which that person will experience thought as a voluntary function and the extent to which that person will have a sense of responsibility for his or her ideas, feelings, and behaviors. A level of consciousness is the degree of understanding of what thought systems are and how they work to shape personal perception, feeling, and behavior.

The particulars of what a person sees and experiences in his or her personal reality is directly related to what that person thinks. Whatever we believe (think) to be happening in our world is what we experience to be true, regardless of whether or not our belief is factual. An anorexic woman believes she is overweight and in her reality she is chubby, even though she only weighs 75 pounds. Similarly, a man who believes that his wife is capable of having an affair may experience the reality of anger and resentment even though his wife is faithful.

When an individual does not recognize that realities are thought-created, that person will experience the reality of what they think, regardless of how untrue, negative, or unpleasant that reality may be. Without the recognition that realities are formed through thought, individuals have the sense that perceptions, feelings, and behaviors are being thrust upon them from some outside source. Without the knowledge of the nature and function of thought, people have no sense of choice or responsibility of what they see, what they feel, and how they act. In other words, they feel at the mercy of the reality that they are creating. However, that individual is less at the mercy of their thought system when they realize how a personal reality is produced and maintained. That realization is a function of that individual's level of consciousness.

Each person lives in a separate reality from every other person. As we discussed previously, this is because each person has a separate and unique system of thinking. The second factor that accounts for separate realities is levels of consciousness. A person's level of consciousness affects the experience of that person's separate reality. This is because a level of consciousness is knowledge one has about the function of thought. Understanding the function of thought shows us that the source of our thinking is within ourselves, and this knowledge gives us a sense of volition in regard to the use of that function. Such knowledge thus directly affects the quality of our reality by determining the degree of objectivity and mobility that we experience within any given reality.

Lower Levels of Consciousness

When people are in lower levels of consciousness, they are caught up in the contents of their thought system with no understanding that what they are perceiving is a direct result of their own thought. For example, Archie Bunker believes that women are inferior, and he mistrusts all minorities. In Archie's personal reality, these beliefs are not seen as thoughts, but as truth. The man has no notion that he is living in a world of his own thinking. He innocently believes that what he personally perceives about the world is an accurate reflection of the way things really are. Archie operates at a low level of consciousness because he sees no connection between his thinking and his reality. He would love to change what he sees but not at the expense of what he thinks! He will argue indefinitely to prove his separate reality as the objective truth, never seeing that it is only his own personal viewpoint.

Unless Archie lets go of his personal beliefs long enough to see that there is more to life than what he thinks, he will never see the existence of separate realities; he will not change his level of consciousness.

Interpersonal, intercultural, and international conflicts result at lower levels of consciousness where people are incapable of seeing beyond their personal reality. While locked into our separate reality, with no understanding that it is a separate reality, we really have no choice other than to analyze, judge, criticize, blame, accuse, agree or disagree, or get into disputes of right or wrong as we go through life using our personal view as the ultimate standard. Only when people step out of their fixed, limited system of thinking, are they are able to see another person, culture, or nation objectively without judgment. They are able to do this because they realize that all human beings are in the same boat because we function in the same way psychologically. This understanding generates compassion rather than conflict. It leads to cooperation rather than coercion and manipulation.

When people are caught in lower levels of consciousness, they will defend their separate reality even though it costs them their feelings of well-being and peace of mind. We give up our mental health when we as individuals, fields of study, or cultures take our thoughts so seriously that we are willing to fight for them. In lower levels of conscious understanding, our thinking tells us that it makes sense to fight. At lower levels of psychological functioning we try in vain to find peace by imposing our beliefs on others. In lower levels of consciousness, it seems to make sense to sacrifice mental health for mental illness, to sacrifice good will for ill will, to sacrifice sanity for insanity.

Lower levels of consciousness are characterized by lack of understanding of how personal reality comes into existence. If a person does not know how realities are made and maintained, he or she will get stuck in realities and not see that there is an alternative. In lower levels of consciousness, a person identifies with a thought system. He or she will tend to react with automatic responses, yet will blame these responses on other people, things, or events in the external situation. This is what happens when a person has little or no sense of volition or responsibility. At higher levels of conscious understanding, things are different because a person begins to realize the connection between thinking and experiencing in life.

Higher Levels of Consciousness

Higher levels of consciousness are healthier states of psychological functioning. At these levels, an individual is able to see his or her reality as resulting from an acquired thought system. With this realization, individuals are free to choose not to respond to this system to create and maintain a negative reality.

A perfect example of this can be seen in the case of Joy, mentioned in the previous chapter. Joy's view of herself as an alcoholic, her perceptions, feelings, and behavior, were all substantiated by the negative memories and experiences of her past because it was true that her parents drank too much, neglected her, and did not provide her with a warm family life. Furthermore, it was true that alcohol had caused Joy a great deal of physical and mental problems. But it was true that Joy had never before glimpsed that it was her constant recollection of those events that kept her stuck in that reality. Once she realized this as a fact, she moved into a higher level of consciousness where she was free from her past.

Joy once told an interesting story in a group session that reflected just how much and how profoundly she had changed via this shift in consciousness. About four months after starting therapy, Joy ran into a very dear friend whom she had not seen since the time both had been in treatment for alcoholism years before. This friend noticed that Joy was happier and healthier than he had ever seen her before. This, however, was not very understandable to him and made him uncomfortable. In the course of asking his friend question after question, he deduced that Joy no longer thought of herself as an "alcoholic." At this point, Joy's friend began reminding her of her past and warning her of the danger of "denying." For a moment, Joy found herself once again thinking of her past and beginning to feel insecure. Joy, however, had already learned too much about thought to blindly repeat her previous mistakes. She quickly realized what was happening and also realized that her well-meaning friend was still living in the same reality (the same level of consciousness) of day-to-day coping that she had known years before. With this recognition, Joy simply changed the subject and began to share her new life with her friend. Incidentally, two months later, Joy's friend asked her for her therapist's name telling her that although he had been initially skeptical by the change he had seen in her, he could no longer deny she had found something substantial. In actuality, what Joy had found was a higher level of consciousness.

Higher levels of consciousness are characterized by feelings of self-esteem, optimism, and happiness. In higher levels people are motivated, productive and creative. These positive feelings exist naturally in higher levels of consciousness; they do not have to be looked for, they do not have to be earned or produced via "positive thinking." In fact, these healthy feelings are an effect or byproduct of a higher level of understanding. They are are not dependent on external situations or events. Regardless of the details of our personal circumstance, in higher levels of consciousness we have an overall sense of well-being and hope for the future. We have a natural feeling of gratitude for the simple pleasures of life and we are able to see the beauty in life. Higher levels of consciousness are states of mental health.

Level of Consciousness and Perception of Reality

As people's level of consciousness diminishes, they become entrenched in their negative view of life and they perceive this view as the only reality that exists. They believe that other people live in exactly the same reality as they do. However, once their level of consciousness begins to rise, people will see that reality is subjective. Their higher level of consciousness will give them the perspective to understand not only their own, but other people's individual realities. Figure 3 illustrates this point. Conflicts and misunderstandings occur when people are locked into their separate realities without having access to the higher psychological vantage point from which to see that there are, in fact, as many separate realities as there are people on earth, some realities being higher and some lower in terms of the degree of understanding life. From this vantage point, people can either chose not to become involved with those who are in lower levels of consciousness and are unwilling to change, or they can see better ways to assist those who are seeking change.

Because of this fact, a shift in the level of consciousness is the central variable involved in process of change. Positive changes in people's experience of life result from a rise in their levels of consciousness. Higher levels bring with them the ability to realize the fact of separate realities and to see how people, including oneself, are causing their own problems by being attached to misconstrued versions of reality. As we shall discuss in subsequent chapters in the context of psychotherapy, the main task of the therapist is to guide his or her clients who honestly want to change, to lessen

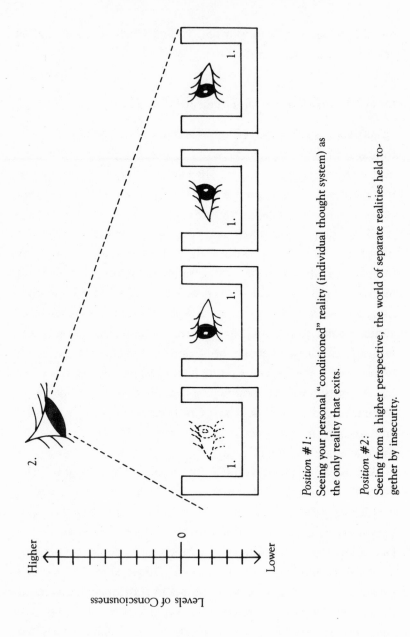

Position #1:
Seeing your personal "conditioned" reality (individual thought system) as the only reality that exits.

Position #2:
Seeing from a higher perspective, the world of separate realities held together by insecurity.

Higher ←—|—|—|—|—|—|—|—|—|—|—|—|—→ Lower

0

Levels of Consciousness

Figure 3

their attachment to their fixed thoughts and views of reality. They will then begin to move to a higher, more objective view where they can see that there is not one, but many realities, none of which are worth being stuck within.

A person's experience of life, the very quality of their reality, fluctuates with his or her conscious level of understanding. A fluctuation in a level of consciousness is what is commonly referred to as a mood. A higher mood is a higher level of understanding, and a low mood is a lower level of understanding. A high mood is a higher level of psychological functioning; a low mood is a decreased or diminished level. A level of consciousness, whether higher or lower, shapes our perception of reality. In higher moods, we are less connected to our conditioned thinking and therefore we see life with increased objectivity. In lower levels, we are caught in the content of our negative thinking without the understanding that it is thinking and that we live in the separate reality produced by that thinking. Low mood thinking perpetuates negative perceptions.

For example, some days, when we are in a higher mood or state of mind, our children are a joy. Everything that they do seems to reflect unusual intelligence or creativity. We enjoy being with them and we feel grateful that we have them in our lives. Let our mood drop, though, and those same children turn into monsters. The children that we adored when we were in a good mood suddenly seem determined to make our life miserable when we are in a bad mood. Everything they do gets on our nerves, and their intelligence seems to drop appreciably. It does no good to talk it over with your spouse, because when you are in a low mood, your spouse doesn't look so good either. Sometimes we are patient and loving, have a sense of humor and take pleasure in our families. Other times, we feel irritable, unfulfilled, and our family seems like a burden. What is the variable that makes the difference?

49

Assuming that our family is simply being themselves, albeit perhaps reacting to the results of our lowered mood, the change that makes the difference in perception and feeling is a shift in our own mood or level of consciousness.

Levels of Consciousness and Separate Realities

Each level of consciousness represents a different reality. We go in and out of different levels of consciousness, or moods, many times even during the course of one day. Thus we experience many different realities. Psychological problems result when people drop into a lower level of consciousness, to activate their conditioned, fearful, or negative beliefs, thereby giving their low level of functioning a realistic form. An individual is then caught in an aversive reality with no understanding of what it is or how to get out of it.

For example, during the course of a day, a counselor may fall into a low state of mind or low level of consciousness. In this separate reality, the counselor's thoughts will be negative and will produce negative perceptions. These perceptions will be viewed as reality. From this lowered, dismal perspective, the clients will appear to be demanding and unresponsive and the caseload will seem overwhelming. It will seem that there is too much to do and not enough time to do it in. From the perspective created by this state of mind, this counselor will think that the other people who work in the clinic are uncooperative and self-serving. It is in these lower levels of consciousness that this clinician will think of exploring other career opportunities. This is the condition many professionals call "burnout."

These are some of the particulars or details that come from conditioned thinking in a low mood. If this counselor began to understand the nature and function of thought, he would realize that he doesn't want to become attached to the negative particulars that result from his low-level thinking, but wants to let them pass so that a higher level of consciousness can be achieved. Once this happens, this counselor will feel better and will view things from an entirely different perspective to perhaps find that he enjoys his work after all.

An awareness of how people move in and out of levels of consciousness is crucial to understanding human behavior. It is important to be able to determine whether we are in a higher or lower level of consciousness at any given moment. The infallible directional guide that lets us know immediately whether our conscious state is high or low is our feelings or emotions.

PRINCIPLE 4: THE ROLE OF FEELINGS AND EMOTIONS AS INDICATORS OF LEVELS OF CONSCIOUSNESS

Since our thought system leads us to think that the world exists literally just the way we view it through our perceptual filters, we must find a way, other than our thinking, to recognize when we are at a lower level of functioning. The key to this recognition is found in an understanding of the role of feelings and emotions.

Feelings as Directional Guides

Every human being knows when he or she is feeling good. Positive feelings of well-being are a human being's innate wisdom and common sense in action. Most people rely on their feelings to guide them through life, but as a rule, they don't know what feelings are. They are unaware that feelings and emotions are simply indicators of a person's state of mind or present level of conscious understanding. Yet it follows logically from the first three principles that feelings are indisputable indicators of a person's level of psychological functioning, whether high or low, at any given point in time. Positive feelings result from higher, more mentally healthy states of mind. Negative feelings, on the other hand, result from lower, more maladaptive levels of consciousness. Negative feelings and emotions are an infallible guide that signal us the moment that our level of understanding drops and we begin to turn that level into a negative reality through our conditioned thinking. Most people have not realized that the role of negative feelings is to alert a person that he or she has dropped into a lower level of psychological functioning. Most people believe that negative feelings are worth thinking about.

There is a prevalent belief in the field of psychology today that negative feelings should be valued, cherished, and passed on to our friends and loved ones. The idea is that negative feelings somehow add depth and substance to our lives and have potential for developing personal character and moral strength. Instead of seeing negative feelings for what they are, which is psychological malfunctioning, we have glorified them and focused on them as the way to achieve mental health. In truth, trying to achieve mental health via negativity is analogous to trying to achieve peace of mind through fighting. It can never be done.

It is believed in the mental health field today that negative feelings are somehow accumulated and stored up somewhere in the human mind or body in such a way that they silently fester and eventually erupt and disrupt our lives. The field not only created this belief about feelings, but it also created the antidote of focusing on negative feelings as a way to "get them out." People are told that in order to feel better they must first feel worse. They must first focus on and intensify their negative feelings in order to "get in touch with" and "release" negative feelings. Quite often, for example, this means that a wife who comes to therapy because she has lost her loving feelings for her husband will be asked to think

52

about, to enumerate, explore, and expand on her resentments, judgments, and insecurities regarding her spouse. If the wife is hesitant to do this, she will be told that she is "blocking," "resist-ing," and "denying" her feelings, and that that is what caused her problem in the first place. So the client will comply and think intently about how bad things are and become even more angry, more isolated, more insecure by dwelling on the thinking that caused her negative feelings to begin with. It would not be difficult for this woman to come to the conclusion that her husband (not her thinking) is causing her so much pain that she has no other choice but to end the relationship.

The unfortunate thing here is that both the client and the therapist have been misled. Negative feelings are not stored up like air in a balloon or pus in an abcess; they are not forced upon us from the outside but they are created moment by moment by thinking at lower levels of consciousness. If the client were told this, she could drop the thinking patterns that are maintaining her negative feelings, and raise her level of consciousness to find her mental health and with it, her loving feelings.

The case of Jeanie provides an example. Jeanie was a 48-year-old mother of three whose husband, Tom, was physically abusive toward her. This abusive pattern had gone on for 19 years. On several occasions, Jeanie required medical attention for lacerations and contusions. Jeanie's problem was that she had adapted to feel-ing insecure. When Tom was in a bad mood, Jeanie's level of understanding was such that she took his negative feelings person-ally. Feeling hurt and insecure, Jeanie would go on the verbal defensive, bringing up things that she knew would get to Tom. These arguments would escalate to the point where Tom would become abusive. Each time this cycle occurred, Jeanie would be-come angry and retaliate. She would fantasize about having an affair and leaving Tom. She would then feel guilty about these thoughts and begin to imagine what life would be like on her own with her three small children, without money or a partner. She would feel justified in feeling anger, hate and resentment. At this level of consciousness, Jeanie saw no real way out of her reality.

At the request of a friend who could see what Jeanie could not, Jeanie began seeing a counselor. Initially, Jeanie thought she was in counseling to get advice on how to leave Tom. Thus, it was not surprising that she found it very difficult to entertain the possibility that her thinking and her feelings played an important role in sustaining her predicament. When Jeanie's level of understanding rose she began to see that her own level of insecurity had led her to actually promote or elicit abuse from her already insecure husband. Later, feeling more secure, Jean was able to get out of the way of Tom's insecurity and protect herself from harm. For example, on one occasion when Tom became violent without any provocation, Jeanie simply took her children to a shelter. She later telephoned Tom and told him how much she loved him but that she would no longer put up with hostility and abuse. She had never done this before and Tom was shocked. Three weeks later, Tom entered counseling. The abuse disappeared from their marriage when this couple began to understand the true nature and results of negative feelings.

As we begin to understand the real significance behind what we feel, we begin to realize that feelings are an internal compass that can guide us past the pitfalls of life, regardless of the details or conditions that exist around us. When we begin to use our feelings simply as directional guides to our level of consciousness, we stop pursuing negative emotions and begin to seek positive feelings. That is the route to mental health.

Positive feelings such as optimism, enjoyment, interest in life, creativity, productivity, and motivation signal that an individual is in a higher level of consciousness. Positive feelings let us know that we are heading in the right direction and that whatever we have to do, we are in a good state of mind to do it. Our chances for success are enhanced, we find simple, common-sense solutions to our problems, and we enjoy what we are doing. In other words, positive feelings are a green light that let us know it is safe to proceed on course. When we are feeling good we are operating at our best. Positive feelings indicate a higher level of psychological functioning.

On the other hand, negative feelings such as irritation, anger, jealousy, boredom, stress, burnout or tension are signs that our level of functioning is below par. When we function at levels at which we generate negative thought, this thought will in turn generate negative feelings. An unpleasant feeling tells us that our level of consciousness is low and so whatever we attempt to do will be unpleasant or difficult and we may not do it well. A negative feeling lets us know that we are at a spinning-our-wheels-but-not-going-anywhere level of functioning. Negativity of any form alerts us that we should slow down and proceed with caution, because psychologically speaking we are literally an accident that is looking for a place to happen. At lower levels of psychological functioning we feel insecure, emotionally off-balance. Our thoughtful concerns are perceived as fixed. Our choices appear to be limited, nonexistent or unpleasant. We are unmotivated and unproductive. These feelings are characteristic of a person in a low level of consciousness.

Feelings, whether positive or negative, are simply indicators of the level of our present psychological functioning. When viewed from this perspective, feelings become resources that we use to keep us oriented on a positive level.

Using the four principles of human psychological functioning that have been presented, we are able to understand the relationships between thought and habits, stress and dysfunctional behavior. We begin to see that we are at the mercy of personality traits, habits, learned behaviors, and insecure states *only* when we do not realize how these things are connected to thought in certain levels of consciousness. As we gain a practical working knowledge of these principles, we are able to regain our power, take responsibility for our own feelings as the effects of our thinking and, therefore, improve the quality of our lives.

CHAPTER FOUR

The Psychology
of Mind
and Mental
Health

When a science does not understand the principles governing its subject matter, it encounters problems when it tries to make sense of its own observations. At these levels of understanding, a science typically produces a great deal of confusion by generating conflicting hypotheses, theories, and predictions. What has become clear to us is that this is precisely the same process of producing conflict that occurs within individual human beings when they do not understand the origins of their own thoughts and perceptions. People, whether they recognize it or not, are engaged in the science of understanding their experience of life. People want to know why things happen the way they do. Human beings want to know why they feel, perceive, and behave in certain ways. They want to know why other people feel, perceive, and behave in certain other ways. People who do not have some degree of understanding of the source of perceptions and feelings must see the world through misconceptions in much the same way as the early astronomers did prior to understanding what they were witnessing. Emotional and perceptual misconceptions are the basis for psychological disorders.

COMMON SENSE

The recognition that thought produces one's perception, feelings, and behavior is what we are calling *common sense*. By common sense we do not mean commonly held beliefs. Common sense is an innate psychological sense. It is a level of understanding that reveals to the individual that his observations are inseparable from his thinking. This common sense resides within each individual as a level of consciousness. The manifestation of common sense is what we would call mental health.

For example, let's consider Bill, who in the absence of understanding thought, has a belief that if his wife, Mary, really loves him she will have dinner ready when he comes home from work. One day, however, Bill arrives home and finds that Mary has gone to the shopping mall with a friend and there is no dinner prepared. In a low level of consciousness, Bill will have no choice but to respond to his belief about what this situation means and he will automatically interpret Mary's absence as a lack of love. Consequently, Bill becomes upset, hurt, even angry and creates a scene when Mary comes home.

Bill initially responds automatically at the effect of his belief, but the next day, after a good night's sleep and feeling rested, he is able to realize that his negative feelings and perception of what happened the previous evening resulted from his interpretation of the event. With this realization, Bill can see that Mary's absence did not mean what he thought it meant. He also can see that if he had been in a good mood, they would have had a pleasant evening together.

The emergence of this more objective, more positive view of reality is the emergence of common sense. The reason why Bill did not access it the previous day is that he did not know that such a thing as common sense existed. Thus he was at the mercy of a barrage of negative interpretations. Common sense teaches the individual that the way out of negativity is through our recognition of where that negativity is coming from—our thinking in a low level of psychological functioning. This recognition is the beginning of stable mental health.

THE DYNAMICS OF MENTAL HEALTH

Before people are able to maintain their mental health, it is necessary for them to understand what mental health is and where it comes from. It is necessary for people to discard the old definitions, beliefs and superstitions to embrace a more factual, comprehensive view. The first thing to be discarded is the idea that mental health is a thought process. This is not true. Mental health per se has nothing to do with the content of people's thinking, their beliefs, concepts, or theories. In other words, mental health is not something that must be produced and sustained by believing, affirming, or denying anything. Mental health exists before, during, and after thinking takes place. Mental health is a state of mind or a level of consciousness.

The states of mental health are characterized by those feelings of well-being and self-esteem that are not contingent on any belief, behavior, or external circumstance. Consequently, mental health does not have to fluctuate depending on what is happening in a person's life situation. Mental health originates internally, in a positive state of mind that is not dependent on anything outside of itself. These states of mind are the psychological conditions of clarity, perspective, and objectivity where one's conditioned thinking does not overshadow one's understanding to create mental disturbances. In these higher states of consciousness, we understand the nature of thought and how it works to create personal reality. When this happens, we are no longer at the effect of our own thinking. We understand how our level of consciousness, in conjunction with our acquired thought system, determines exactly what is happening in our lives psychologically at any given moment. At such levels of understanding, common sense shows us obvious ways to maintain sanity or mental health.

Since mental health is a level of consciousness, it cannot be lost. This raises an interesting question. If mental health cannot be lost, then what are mental disorders? Very simply, mental disorders are instances in which the individual becomes absorbed by the content of his or her negative thinking at a level of consciousness where that individual is not aware that they are thinking. Functioning at these levels of consciousness means that the thinker's reality will be predominantly determined by the content of his or her thinking to the exclusion of the fact that the content is thought created. Consequently, the thinker experiences a reality of negative feelings and perceptions and ascribes these to an external reality rather than as attributes of the content of thinking originating within himself. Simply stated, people at this level of functioning consider their experiences in life as existing independent of thought. The result is that the experiencer tries to comprehend his or her predicament by thinking about how to get out of it. In doing so, a vicious cycle is initiated wherein the thinker unknowingly sustains the negative reality simply by keeping it alive in his thinking. This is the psychological basis of mental disorders. But even in this case, mental health is not lost. It is still present, but obscured by the contents generated by a negative thinking process. Remember, people in this predicament try to think their way out of their problems, believing that their feelings and perceptions are a result of some external condition. These people may have no understanding that negative feelings are indicators that a person is thinking in a psychologically compromised state. The vicious cycle of mental disturbance does not stop until that trend of thought is stopped. However, the moment the individual stops generating negative thoughts, relief is experienced immediately. Once again, this is because mental health is always present but can only be discerned in the absence of negative thinking.

Mental disorders, then, are vicious cycles of insecure thinking that result in negative feelings, perceptions, and behaviors. Yet the very moment an individual's level of consciousness rises and the thinker drops his or her negative thought processes, that individual finds some degree of immediate emotional, perceptual, and behavioral relief. Figure 4 illustrates the two possible cycles of psychological functioning that characterize mental health and mental disorder.

For example, most of us have had the experience of having a problem on our minds. We think about it over and over again and we talk about it with our friends and acquaintances. All the time we are thinking about the problem or talking about it, we are feeling the effects of it. However, if we get distracted from our thoughts and get absorbed in something else, perhaps an unexpected pleasant conversation with a friend, we drop the thought of the problem. The second that we drop the thought of the problem, the moment that we take our attention off it, the problem, for all practical purposes, disappears. For that period of time we are free of it. It is forgotten.

When something is forgotten, it means that it does not exist in our minds, and if it does not exist in our minds, it does not exist in our reality. It is like forgetting your three o'clock dental appointment. Three o'clock comes and goes and as far as you are concerned, the dental appointment does not exist. Only later, when you remember it once again, does it exist for you.

Human beings have a natural ability to disengage themselves from pointless thinking. For example, what happens to a family that is having a terrible fight, yelling, screaming, blaming, crying, when Aunt Tillie and Uncle Tom arrive from out of town? The family immediately puts on their best behavior. In order to do this, they must forget their fight. In this case, they were motivated to drop the thinking that was keeping the argument alive because they wanted to look a certain way for the company. Another time,

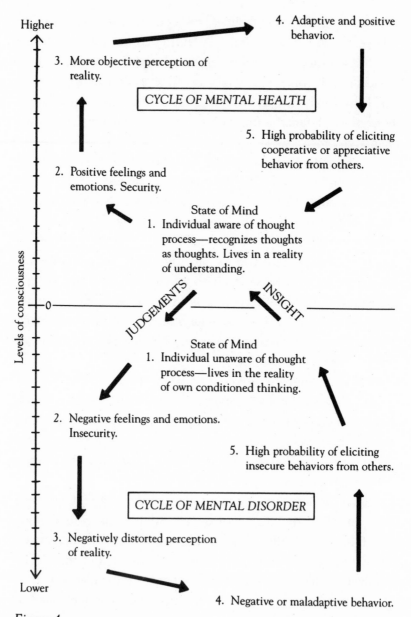

Figure 4

Cycles of Mental Health and Disorder

if someone with common sense had said to these people, drop the thought of the fight and it will be gone, these people may well have responded, "We'd like to stop fighting, but we just can't stop thinking about it." In truth, we can stop thinking about anything. If we are thinking about it, we can just as easily *not* think about it. We drop thoughts all the time but are not aware of what we are doing.

The normal human being typically believes that a problem has been resolved by the passage of time, some ritual, or external change. What people rarely recognize is the fact that they themselves stopped producing their problem by dropping it from thought and that this is what has brought their well-being back into conscious recognition. Thus even though people do in fact regain some degree of mental health when they drop their conditioned negative thinking, their lack of understanding that this is what gave them relief, makes it almost impossible to hold on to mental health. Consequently, the cycle repeats itself either in the form of blatant psychological disorders or in what are called "bad" moods.

MOODS AND MENTAL HEALTH

No matter who we are, we all go in and out of states of mental health. These normative fluctuations in one's mental health are what people call "moods." We are not accustomed to viewing moods in this way because we are not accustomed to seeing that "normal" people may sometimes lack mental health or that "abnormal" people may sometimes be mentally healthy. Thus moods are fluctuations in our level of psychological functioning and they occur along a continuum.

In higher moods or higher mental states (or higher levels of consciousness), a person is operating at a higher level of psychological functioning. Higher states are characterized by positive feelings, self-esteem, well-being, motivation, objectivity, creativity, productivity, and good humor. In these states of mind people have a greater appreciation of themselves, their families, their friends, and their work. Higher moods are levels of consciousness where stress is minimal or nonexistent and people have a sense of hopefulness and optimism about the future. In higher moods, people have more mental health and thus a greater understanding of their ability to think. In higher states, all these qualities are naturally present and are not dependent on the circumstances of life.

For example, Jan, a nurse, in a good mood herself and with an understanding of moods as levels of psychological functioning, was talking to Sam, a patient with an incurable disease who had just been readmitted to the hospital and was feeling depressed. In his state of insecurity, Sam was demanding, reactive, and critical of the care that was being offered to him. Instead of reacting to the patient's insecurity, Jan felt a great deal of compassion for Sam and ten minutes later, Sam had calmed down considerably and Jan decided to spend some extra time with him, helping him to calm down. Jan gently explained to the patient that he was understandably experiencing a low mood. She suggested that he watch some television and get some rest, and that he would feel better in the morning when his mood came up. The next morning Jan saw Sam walking down the hall with a smile on his face. He was teasing the nurses and having a good time. He told Jan how grateful he was to know that his bad feelings were simply a low mood and nothing more. He was very relieved to know that he could go through his illness with some degree of mental health.

Moods are variations in reality and in higher levels people realize that they can improve the quality of how they experience life.

Human beings function differently in higher states of mind because their view of reality has shifted to a different level. At higher levels, the content of thought takes a secondary role and allows the individual's well-being to emerge. Thus an individual functioning in a "good" mood or higher level of mental health will be able to view situations in life with more clarity and understanding. A person in a high mood may take a firm stand on certain things, but this person will do so with compassion and respect for everyone involved. A person in a higher level is open to new ideas and is able to be creative. In these states of mind, a person can see the bigger picture and is able to achieve positive results.

When an individual drops into a low mood, that person's insecure thinking becomes compelling because that is all he is conscious of. It is at these levels that a person becomes controlled by his beliefs, by his conditioning from the past. In lower moods, a person has forgotten that he is the one who is producing the thought, and so he takes negative thoughts seriously. He relies exclusively on his conditioned view of life to solve the problem those views created in the first place. Of course, this does not work. Lower levels of understanding or lower moods are characterized by the presence of self-consciousness, seriousness, and negative feelings. In these states of mind, individuals are not in contact with their mental health. They are unaware of their thinking as the formulator of reality. In these levels of consciousness, an individual becomes insecure; that is, he becomes anxious, worried, upset, or stressed. When a person becomes insecure, he feels overwhelmed by life. It seems either that there is not enough time to get things done, or else it seems that there is too much time and not enough to do. Life seems very serious and the individual loses a sense of humor. Family, friends, and work lose their appeal as he loses his zest for life.

As was mentioned earlier, we are not accustomed to viewing

"low" or "bad" moods as psychological malfunctioning, but they are. Low moods are the normal or socially sanctioned excursions into the realm of mental disorders. If a low mood becomes intensified or prolonged beyond what is considered normal, then it is labeled a mental disorder. In other words, mental health and mental disorders lie along a single continuum. This is most helpful to understand because it is from a baseline of normal moods that we launch ourselves into agony or ecstasy.

THOUGHT AND MENTAL HEALTH

Every person develops a thought system that includes how they should react to different types of events and problems. The ability to see beyond one's own beliefs culminates in the presence of mental health. Mental disorders are experienced when we cannot see beyond the boundaries of our own subjective frame of reference (a perspective that is personal, but seems absolute to us). Our subjective frame of reference cannot impart understanding to us, the thinkers. It cannot tell us how we work psychologically. A frame of reference or a system of thinking is simply arbitrary programming. We can only access from it what we put into it to begin with—information. A thought system is incapable of providing psychological understanding.

It is understanding that determines the way in which one's own thinking is experienced. Anyone who realizes understanding to the degree we are calling common sense can see the complications people create for themselves when they attempt to help themselves by analyzing their problems, their pasts, their personalities, their habits, their relationships, or other people. This process is contaminated from the beginning. It is this very process that manifests itself in mental disorders.

Our thought system is capable of handling an incredible variety of tasks. We use it for remembering our language, balancing our checkbook, driving a car, or finding our way to and from work. But while our thought system is impressive for these tasks, it is not an infallible interpreter of life. To interpret life, we hope to access or use our understanding, common sense, wisdom, or whatever name we wish to give the ability to see beyond our conditioned interpretations of life. The reason these are not accessed as frequently as we would like is that understanding or mental health is confused with the content of what we think. Understanding, however, is a dimension that exists separate from the content of our biased thought system. This means that we cannot think our way to wisdom. This is why relief from one's own misunderstandings always seems to come unexpectedly, usually in the form of an insight, inspiration, or realization. It comes in the form of seeing an obvious, simple, common-sense solution without the process of mental or intellectual struggle. Understanding and insight involve seeing beyond our personal frame of reference.

FEELINGS AND MENTAL HEALTH

Every negative feeling that we experience as human beings comes about as a direct result of our thinking. That is, a negative feeling indicates that we have lost sight of the most basic thing that we are doing, which is thinking. We are thinking at a level of consciousness where our own negative thought patterns are being mistaken for reality. Once we begin to observe this thinking process with objectivity, without becoming entangled in the content, we see how to stop using our thinking function against ourselves. Once this relationship is understood as a fact, achieving lasting mental health is simplicity itself.

There is a reality that is deeper than what a human being creates through personal thought. Until this larger reality is discerned, all of a person's life experiences will continue to be derived from and limited to the personal, conditioned thought system. This means that a person will be at the effect of this system of thinking no matter how ill-conceived it may be or how adverse the effects of it are to that person's mental health and well-being. The way out of this system cannot be found by thinking. That is, one cannot ask the system to show the way out of itself. The system is simply incapable of directing attention outside of itself.

The way to the larger reality does not involve more thinking. Rather, the way to see the bigger picture involves becoming more conscious of the fact that there is a reality beyond what we think. At the point that we have this recognition, we can begin to consciously withdraw our support from negative, insecure thought patterns, allowing our mental health to reemerge. A recognition of the fact that we are thinking and that thinking creates feelings, perceptions, and behaviors is what allows us to direct this function in more positive, productive, and creative ways.

What we are looking for—mental health—is not reached through intellectualization, mental struggle, or thought processes, but through positive feelings. This is the source and nature of mental health. Positive feelings lead us to states of mind where we function psychologically at a higher level. At these levels we can see our own role in the production of our personal reality. This allows us to view our situation with more perspective, objectivity, and common sense.

KNOWLEDGE AND MENTAL HEALTH

The psychological principles that we have introduced in this book are the stepping-stones that will help the science of mental health and the individual to understand the relationship between thought and perception. This understanding will help bring into recognition the fact that human beings are the effect of their pasts, their personality traits, their beliefs, their theories, and their conditioning, *only* when those human beings are not conscious of the fact that these things are all connected to and derived from their own thinking. As people gain an understanding of this fact, they begin to realize their responsibility for the effects of their thinking. This is what clears the way for them to recognize their power and regain the ability to change the quality of their thinking, feelings, perceptions, and behaviors.

These principles have important implications for the field of psychology. The principles point away from theories and models that focus on the effects of human psychological functioning (the details of perceptions, feelings, or behaviors) rather than on the fact of the functioning itself. Present-day theories and treatment models have overlooked the fact that negative feelings result from the maladaptive use of thought. This oversight is analogous to developing surgical treatment overlooking the fact of microbiological contamination. In both of these situations, crucial data has been overlooked and the techniques that would be applied, by even the most sincere practitioner, would introduce contamination into their interventions. In subsequent chapters we will discuss how this oversight has led to the development of psychotherapies that lead people deeper into their problems in an effort to find mental health. Contaminated results are unavoidable when the frame of reference of psychology assumes that psychological problems are anything other than an effect of the individual's level of consciousness and thinking in the present moment. When the field of psychology formally recognizes the relationship between thought and reality, it will be able to guide people directly back to mental health.

CHAPTER FIVE

Insecurity

Every human being, regardless of age, sex, culture, nationality, IQ, or profession, has experienced the feeling of insecurity. Insecurity is a feeling that many of us have known too well and understood too little. It is this lack of understanding that has allowed insecurity to become an integral and unrecognized part of our daily lives. In this chapter we will explain the origin and nature of insecurity as it relates to psychological functioning and mental health.

Previously, we established that the feelings that people experience emerge directly as a byproduct of their thinking. Further, these feelings are indicative of the level of psychological functioning or mental health. However this is not the way most people perceive feelings. Individuals normally think, and thus perceive, that what they are feeling is a result of, or is being mediated by something outside themselves, such as other people, conditions, or situations. Thus even when happiness is present, the normal human being is never really secure because he does not know where his well-being is coming from, what it represents, or how to keep it. This level of understanding is the breeding ground for insecurity.

Insecurity is the feeling of fear that emerges from the acceptance of a thought that something outside of us will somehow harm us, take away our well-being, and strip us of our self-esteem. While we have all felt this uncomfortable feeling, most of us have not recognized that the true source of this feeling is our own thinking, or that its presence signifies a reduction in our level of functioning. This is because the thoughts that create insecurity invariably point to some external cause for its existence. Thus in the absence of understanding what thought is and how it works, we are forced to indiscriminately look outside ourselves to find the solution for our insecurities. We have no choice but to accept and live in the separate reality that is created by our conditioned form of thinking and experience of life. We have no choice but to prove, defend, and attempt to impose our separate reality on others. This attempt only serves to increase the feeling of insecurity and lead us to adhere even more dogmatically to whatever misunderstood beliefs produced our insecure feelings in the first place.

What does it mean to feel insecure? First of all, it means that one is experiencing a negative feeling. It also means that it is time to take an honest look to see if the feeling we are experiencing is common sense or nonsense. If we are standing in the middle of a road and see a truck coming at us, we will naturally have the thought that we are in danger. This thought will create a feeling of fear that tells us to get out of the way. This is common sense. However, if we are fearful of going grocery shopping because we are afraid that we will get run over by a truck, this is insecurity. Insecurity is nonsense.

THE SIDE EFFECTS OF INSECURITY

One way people become more sane is to realize that insecurity is a thought. It is produced in thinking prior to its emergence in any particular feeling form, or context. Because of separate realities, each person's insecurity (or security) will emerge in a different form. Some people may focus their insecurity on their jobs, others will focus it on relationships. For others, this feeling may emerge as anger toward a parent or against society. Whatever form this feeling takes, it is not a pleasant experience. People who have high degrees of insecurity try to deal with these feelings in a variety of ways. Some try to change another person (or the world) to conform to their belief system. Others attempt to numb insecure feelings and thoughts by using alcohol or drugs. Some people try to escape the feeling through proving themselves, being workaholics; others express insecurity through aggressive, angry behavior or through depression and withdrawal. Some people turn to excessive stimulation and whirlwind activity; others become immobilized and nonproductive. Compulsive or habitual behavior in any form is a result of insecurity. Overeating and undereating have the same underlying cause—unrecognized thoughts and feelings of insecurity.

It is important to realize that insecurity is behind all destructive or maladaptive behavior. When we begin to understand how this feeling sustains habitual or compulsive behaviors, we begin to see the value in dropping insecure thoughts to eliminate this negative feeling at its source. At the point that we drop thoughts of insecurity we are able to relax, feel more secure, and find increased enjoyment in life. Once we begin to see how insecurity works to perpetuate itself, we are able to break the patterns that keep us attached to it. Then we are on the way to a more emotionally stable, less stressful, and happier life. This is true regardless of the external situation. Self-destructive behaviors begin to drop away when we realize their connection to insecure thinking.

Take the example of Vicki, a mother who was preoccupied with her children's psychological normality. Vicki, a child psychologist, was a very insecure woman, especially about being thought of by her friends and acquaintances as an inadequate mother. After all, she was supposed to be an expert. Vicki had an enormous intellectual storehouse of concepts about what could go awry in children, when normal children are supposed to be able to do certain tasks, become socially conscious, and so on.

The first sign of trouble was seen by the school staff at the day care center that Vicki's two and four-year-old children, Laura and June, attended. The teachers noticed that both girls were manifesting a great deal of anxiety toward the parents of other children. Also, when the Humane Society brought puppies and kittens for the children to play with, Laura and June became very frightened of the animals. When the teachers described this behavior to Vicki, she became frightened. She told the teachers that she was worried that Laura was not cautious enough with strangers and was afraid the child would be hurt because of this. It didn't take long for the staff to begin to notice that these children were reacting to their mother's insecurity. They noticed that Vicki would drop the children off in the morning, admonishing them at the door to be cautious of strangers. Vicki hinted at lurking danger, abduction, and sexual abuse. She warned her children daily of the danger of being bitten by unfamiliar dogs or cats. Each afternoon, when Vicki would pick up her children, she had a list of clinical questions for the teachers. Were Laura and June "appropriate"? Were they acting normal? Did they show signs of group affiliation?

The staff noticed that during the first part of the morning, Laura and June were frightened and insecure to the point that they did not listen to the teachers. Yet as the morning progressed, these two little girls would settle down, drop their insecurity, and become healthy and happy children. In the afternoon when Vicki would arrive to pick them up, their behavior would change instantly and, once again, they would be tense and nervous. The teachers could see that the girls were reacting to their mother's fear. They were responding to Vicki's seriousness and intensity. Thus the more Vicki tried to counter her children's reactions, the more reactions she had to work with.

The teachers could see what was happening. They gently suggested to Vicki that she relax, enjoy being a mother and set aside her theories and unnecessary fears. Luckily, Vicki was willing to listen. Although Vicki was too insecure to talk to another psychologist about her own fears, she nonetheless listened to the common sense that the teachers imparted so that she was able to set aside her fear-filled thoughts and find a healthier, more secure state of mind for herself. Over the succeeding months, the staff saw an unbelievably beautiful change not only in Vicki, but in her children, as well.

Vicki is an example of a person who experiences insecurity as a result of her thought that an external situation is the cause of the problem. In a low mood of insecurity, this mother's thinking would lead her to see her children's misbehavior as having not only extremely serious psychological implications, but also would make her feel insecure about herself as a professional. Following this line of thought, Vicki would lose her feeling of well-being and blame this loss on her youngsters' behavior. In this state of mind, she did not realize that her perception was being shaped by her thinking in a low mood. She believed that she was seeing things as they really are, and in her thoughts at that level there was no other reality. This misguided perception only served to increase her insecurity as a mother and a professional. Not seeing her own role in the production of her negative feelings, she was forced to believe that her happiness hinged on the behavior of her children. This belief would cause any parent to be insecure.

Regardless of how it appeared to Vicki, *insecurity is a product of thinking in a low state of mind.* Because it is thought, the feeling of insecurity is created moment to moment. Insecurity is a direct product of human psychological functioning. The issue is not what circumstances a person has in his or her life, but rather, how that individual's thinking has shaped those circumstances. Regardless of what we have learned in the past, thinking results in feelings. Human beings run into difficulties when they do not realize the role that thinking plays in what they are feeling and perceiving at the moment.

As we have indicated throughout this book, each individual

wants to know how to effect positive change. Yet before a positive shift takes place, it is necessary to recognize the psychological barriers to change. The factor that keeps anyone's thoughts in a fixed configuration is the insecurity that is generated by thinking. Once a person feels insecure, they are in a state of mind where it is difficult to change because any change appears to be threatening and upsetting to them.

Problems result when a person views his situation from a level of consciousness involving insecurity. If a person does not feel insecure, he will not view his situation as problematic. If he feels insecure, any situation has the potential to be perceived as a problem. Insecurity is the common denominator that serves as the basis for defensiveness, anger, jealousy, fear, boredom, stress, greed, envy, grief, or sorrow. Feelings of insecurity can be generalized and nonspecific, as in the form of generalized anxiety, or they can be focused specifically on other people, places, or things, or even on oneself. When insecurity is not recognized for what it is, it becomes the nucleus of mental, social, and international dysfunction.

RECOGNIZING INSECURITY

Understanding insecurity helps us understand how our thought systems are activated and maintained. To understand how insecurity works, we must look at it before it manifests into any particular form of nervousness, self-consciousness, fear, phobia, anxiety, or other mental problem. *Understanding how insecure thought creates the feeling of insecurity is the most important realization on the road to mental health.* Feelings of insecurity keep a human being from experiencing his or her own well-being, self-esteem, emotional maturity, and mental health. Insecurity replaces natural

80

good feelings, clarity, and common sense, and obscures good judgment, motivation, and interest in life. This is true at home, work, or play.

For example, let's look at what insecurity does to sports. Everyone who has played a sport realizes that when we have no worry, no conscious thought about how well we are doing, when we aren't using our thinking process to figure out every move, we naturally do well. However, as soon as we start thinking too much about the game and our own performance, we become self-conscious and we lose our natural knowing or intuitive feel for the game.

John played high school basketball but was not good enough to play in college. At one point in graduate school, he was invited to play a pick-up game with some friends, all of whom had played college basketball. In this situation, John began to think about his ability in comparison with the others, and he felt insecure about his ability to play well enough to earn their approval. He became self-conscious and tried to think out every move in advance in order to do well. The more he tried to look good, the worse he played. His passes went out of bounds, he lost the ball, and his shots missed the basket completely. At one point, John decided that things were so bad that he just gave up trying to prove himself and decided to make the best of it and enjoy the remainder of the game. All of a sudden, when he was not worrying about his game and thinking about doing well, his passes improved, he made good moves, and his shots began to score.

The point is that if we have some understanding that the feeling of insecurity is a result of thinking at a low level of psychological functioning, we can voluntarily begin to cease creating such thinking, or to disengage from this kind of thinking and begin to feel better. The instant the feeling of insecurity vanishes we begin to rediscover our own inner well-being and mental health. Then we are able to once again utilize our thinking to accomplish what we have wanted without effort, stress, or anxiety. Without thoughts of insecurity, we do something simply for the pleasure of doing it. We begin to move toward those things that we truly enjoy in life, those things that we naturally do well. We begin to discover intrinsic satisfaction in our accomplishments, not caring so much about what others think. Learning to recognize and drop insecure thinking is the route to mental health. Any insecure feeling is an immediate and infallible sign that we are in a lower level of psychological functioning. Recognizing our negative feelings as an indicator of a drop in a level of consciousness, we are aware that our thinking is putting us in a psychologically compromised position. With this recognition we are able to move directly into states of mental health.

HOW WE LEARN INSECURITY

Insecurity can contaminate all areas of life. The reason that insecurity is so pervasive is that we have not recognized or realized what thinking is in relation to our level of consciousness. As a result, we have promoted a version of life that is founded on thinking that everyone lives in the same reality. We are taught that in order to be good, worthwhile, or successful, we must believe a certain way, value certain things, and reject certain other things irrespective of the effect that such beliefs have on the quality of our life. Our images of self-importance, our egos, become attached to these beliefs and certain feelings and behaviors logically follows as a result. We learn to go through life, not enjoying ourselves and living naturally at our best, but proving ourselves. We start to prove ourselves in kindergarten when our parents pass along their insecurity about whether we will be as good as the other children. We silently pick up the feeling and set about to prove that we are,

we hope, as good as the others. All the time we are proving ourselves, we have the underlying feeling that we really aren't as good
as everyone else, so we have to work harder for the same accomplishments. We attach our feelings of self-esteem and well-being
to certain things, and when these things don't go as we think, we
lose our good feelings. We can also lose our good feelings when
things are going according to our plan because even when we are
on top we have to stay vigilant and on guard to maintain our
position. With the feeling of insecurity, even when we are successful, we have the nagging feeling that we have to keep our guard
up or things could change. Catering to thoughts of insecurity, a
human being can never win. Even when that human being is
successful by every standard, that person's insecure thoughts will
constantly demand more; more money, more acclaim, more love,
more accomplishments.

When a person is in an insecure state of mind, he or she can
achieve only contingent and thus temporary feelings of satisfaction
or accomplishment. Insecurity will not allow an individual to rest.
Rather, this negative feeling compels people to drive themselves
on and on in search of things to do in order to feel good. For
example, take the student who finds he has one of the highest
grade point averages in his class. After being momentarily pleased
that he has done so well, this student begins to worry about
whether he will be able to maintain his position. This worry turns
the situation from one of pleasure in accomplishment to one of
fear of failure.

Accomplishments do not make people happy. Feelings of happiness, security, pleasure, and enjoyment are what stand behind
worthwhile accomplishments. Yet our thoughts will persist in telling us that there is value in the feeling of insecurity, that there is
value in the feeling of stress. Regardless of what we have learned,
insecurity and worry are not a source of motivation or a sign of

responsibility. Contrary to what most parents believe, worry does not equal caring. In fact, worry equals insecurity, stress, mental blocks, and decreased productivity.

LOVE VERSUS INSECURITY

Once a person begins to drop insecure thought patterns, he or she begins to know the experience of love. Locked into lower, insecure states of mind, an individual may feel sexual gratification, attachment, or need. Some people take these feelings as love, but the true, more profound feeling of love exists only in higher states of mind where there is no insecurity. It is an impossibility to experience the feeling of love and the feeling of insecurity at the same moment. Love and fear are mutually exclusive feelings. Love is a feeling that exists naturally in the absence of insecurity. Love is not a feeling that one has to seek. In higher levels of psychological functioning, this beautiful feeling is simply present as a result or byproduct of higher consciousness.

In the absence of fear, self-consciousness, or negative beliefs, a human being will experience feelings of love, appreciation, contentment, satisfaction, and fulfillment. In the feeling state that we call love, a human being has no ill-conceived or negative desires, needs, demands, or expectations. What does exist is a truly beautiful appreciation for life that is a natural expression of a person's state of mental health. People in insecure states of mind cannot experience the feeling of love because they are too busy proving themselves or judging others.

The feeling of love emerges when a human being is secure in the realization of his own inner mental health. Love is a byproduct of the state of mental health. Love is not really contingent on any external person, place, or thing. This is why it is impossible for one person to give another person the feeling of love. Love is a feeling that wells up from inside. When we do not realize the actual source of our feelings, we look outside ourselves for the justification of our feeling. This is an illusion created by thinking that leads us to look for love in places where it cannot be found. When we know that love is our own mental health, that it is innate, that we were born with unlimited capacity for this feeling, we are able to take responsibility for our own feelings. When we learn the truth of our own psychological functioning, we see that love is a feeling that we give to ourselves.

We can learn something of the feeling of love by looking at the experience that we call "falling in love." At some point in our lives we meet a person and experience a wonderful feeling. In other words, we fall in love. The feeling is so wonderful and so encompassing that the details of each other's beliefs, lifestyles, and backgrounds are irrelevant. So in the context of our discussion of thought, separate realities, levels of consciousness and feelings, the phenomenon of falling in love represents a relative detachment from one's thought system as a result of a rise in one's level of consciousness. This rise is *felt* as an extraordinarily enlivening and positive feeling. The enjoyable feelings that we have are so appreciated, that we set aside any personal beliefs or details that may detract from that good feeling. If our beloved is 30 minutes late, the minute that they arrive, we are so happy to see them that we forget about the wait. Time means nothing when we are together. We happily lose sleep staying up late night after night to be together. We think nothing of driving 100 miles just so we can be with this person. Our pleasure is to do things for each other. We even enjoy doing things that we have not enjoyed doing before. In love, we are thrilled to do the dishes if we can be near our beloved. Even the most simple, ordinary things are pleasurable when we do them in the feeling of love. People in love are immune to problems. A dingy apartment becomes the garden of Eden. The job that was once merely tolerated now takes on new meaning as the financial support for the relationship. Worries fade away in the feelings of gratitude and pleasure of being together.

Most of us are familiar with this experience. Unfortunately, we are also familiar with the events that follow once our insecure thinking begins to replace our loving feelings. Beautiful relationships are destroyed when the partners start thinking about the relationship and analyzing how well it is going. Do we have the same goals? Are my expectations being realized? Are my needs being fulfilled? Is my sweetheart faithful now and forever? Who loves the most? Am I getting my share? What did he mean by that remark? Do I really love her? Does she really love me? Am I a good lover? Is he a good lover? Maybe I should have stayed with that other relationship? Have I made a mistake? Eventually, people move away from willing and effortless feeling and love and replace it with a caravan of conditioned beliefs, opinions, assumptions, expectations, and rituals. The feelings of love are replaced by thoughts of evaluation.

One issue that our thinking raises in relationships is the issue of compatibility. Yet all that compatibility means is whether or not we can tolerate another person's belief system. This issue arises only when we are experiencing life almost entirely from our belief system. Incompatibility is measuring and judging another person's lifestyle and habits against one's own separate reality. Judgment and measurement occur when a person becomes insecure. The amount of incompatibility that people will experience will be directly in proportion to their level of insecurity. On the other hand, if love is present on the part of two people, compatibility is unavoidable. The bottom line is that in the absence of love, nobody is compatible with anyone else.

INSECURITY AND RELATIONSHIPS

Insecurity is the source of conflict in relationships. This is true whether the relationships are between sweethearts, parent and child, friends, workers, nations or cultures. Conflict in relationships occurs when people attempt to impose their personal thought system, their personal reality, on others, without an understanding that other people have separate frames of reference. When friends first meet they do not notice the other person's habits or behavioral patterns. These behaviors are not focused on initially because they do not seem to be important. The feelings of enjoyment are primary at this point. However, the loving feelings become secondary as each person's own separate reality re-emerges. It is then that people begin to notice and highlight their differences. They begin to think about what they like and what they don't like about the other and they start to make these thoughts important and significant. The feelings of pleasure and enjoyment begin to recede as they are replaced by judgment. The degree to which a person in a relationship has activated a conditioned thought system is the degree to which they feel insecure and dissatisfied. The greater the degree of insecurity present in an individual's thought, the more he or she will react with negativity when another person does something out of context with that individual's separate reality.

When a person in a relationship is insecure, he or she will react negatively to situations which, in a healthier state of mind, would not be experienced as threatening. That is why people fight over seemingly insignificant issues. "You always slam the door when you come into the room. Is that necessary? Didn't anyone ever teach you the proper way to come into a room?" The issue here is not doors. The issue is not noise or upbringing. The issue is *negativity*

87

caused by insecure thinking. A person who is feeling secure will probably not even hear the sound of the door, or if they do hear it, they will look up in pleasant expectation to see who has come in.

When a person is in a lower level of consciousness, feeling a high degree of insecurity, he will feel scared and threatened. In this state of mind he will blame other people or situations as being "wrong." This is the way that it looks to a person in a lower state of mind. If a person in a lower mood has no understanding of how realities are formed, he will believe his own thought that something outside him is wrong. That person will then act on this belief and will create some degree of conflict. In lower levels of consciousness, people blame one another for their lack of good feeling. The truth is that insecure thinking is the disguised villain. When people do not realize the source of their insecurity, they judge and react to other people through their own perceptual filters, filters which validate their insecure view.

Once a person in a relationship begins to drop insecure thought patterns, he or she automatically begins to feel secure. It is not difficult to feel secure. The difficult part is to have the courage to drop insecure thought. However, once an insecure reality is dropped, a person naturally moves into another reality, one with a higher degree of security. At this point that person will see the futility of judgments, reactions, blaming, impatience, and fear. This person will have the perspective to realize that conflicts are separate thought systems clashing with each other.

For example, consider the couple who had recurring patterns of conflict in the area of giving advice. Bob had the belief that when someone gave him advice it was because that person felt that he was incapable of running his own life. Susan, on the other hand, believed that giving advice was a gesture of caring and friendship. Regardless of their different beliefs, these people had insecurity in common, so they reacted to one another's beliefs. Their pattern of insecurity went like this: Susan would give Bob advice, thinking that he would appreciate it. Bob, in turn, believing that Susan was putting him down, would get angry and upset. Before long, this couple would be engaged in a fight, and neither of them would realize that the cause of the fight was that each person was defending a separate reality. If Bob were not feeling insecure, he would realize that Susan's intention was not to put him down, but to help him. He would have the objectivity to realize that she was attempting, in her own way, to give him something of value. Without insecurity to obscure his perception, Bob would see beyond the details to realize the feeling of giving. Once he saw this, he would be able to appreciate her gesture.

When people drop thoughts of insecurity, they begin to move to higher levels of consciousness. As a result of this rise in consciousness, they see other people in a more positive, loving, and appreciative way. As people drop insecure thoughts, the enjoyable, exciting feelings of love begin to emerge. They are able to see that other people's habits, reactions, and insecurities are as innocent as their own. Individual behavioral patterns become less and less relevant as people stop evaluating and analyzing, take responsibility for their own feelings and start to enjoy life. The most natural state of relationships is one of appreciation. This grows deeper as we find out how personal thought leads us to feelings of insecurity.

The secret to having satisfying, enjoyable relationships is not in learning techniques of parenting, communication, or behavior modification. All that we need to do to improve our relationships is to drop insecure thoughts and allow our natural warmth and understanding to emerge. This is what happened to Vicki. Once she experienced feelings of love and respect for her children, she was naturally able to guide her girls to their own security.

All we need to do to improve our relationships, whether with our spouses, our children, friends, or coworkers, is to drop our insecurity. In the absence of insecurity we have more objectivity, more common sense, understanding, and wisdom. We see creative, cooperative, and loving ways to handle the differences that will always exist between people who live in separate realities. The secret to a happy relationship is to be a happy person. This happens when we desire happiness above the need to prove ourselves or to be right. A person frequently faces the choice of whether to be right or to be happy. It is their choice, their free will. We can go through life being right if that is our goal, but what is sacrificed is our happiness.

THE FREEDOM BEYOND INSECURITY

When we drop insecurity we are able to see the wisdom in choosing happiness over being right or proving ourselves. We are able to do this because we understand our own basic psychological functioning. With this understanding, other people's separate realities will not affect us negatively because we can see how they are thought-created. We can recognize when people are innocently caught up in their thought-created reality with no idea of what is happening. By maintaining our own security and well-being, we are able to stay outside of this reality. When we are not caught up maintaining and defending our personal reality, we are able to add sanity to the situation rather than adding to the insanity.

The number one antidote for insecurity is the natural state of happiness or mental health. The positive feelings that come from these higher states of mind are what quiet down the thought process. The feelings of mental health are not associated with or contingent upon any condition or outcome. Since these feelings are noncontingent, they cannot be attained by doing something or proving ourselves. They cannot be attained through any technique or process. States of mental health come when individuals begin to live outside their conditioned thought system and give up trying to figure out or to solve problems from a level of consciousness that produces insecurity.

The path to mental health is to learn to recognize and drop insecurity as if it were the plague, because it is the plague to mental health. The key to dropping insecurity is to realize that this feeling is not useful and is simply a product of conditioned, habitual thought patterns which we accept and maintain by our attention to these beliefs. Any thought that a human being creates, a human being can reject or drop. Once we do this, negative feelings are neutralized and we find ourselves in higher levels of consciousness, enjoying life without fear. We begin to see life through positive feelings that come from within and are not unduly tied to external events. Thus we begin to perceive a reality of life that neither has the power to make us feel good nor deny us happiness.

CHAPTER SIX

Ego

When people do not realize that they are thinking or what thinking is, they unknowingly use their thought system to create an image of who they believe they are. This thought-created image is what has been called the "ego" or self. In essence, this means that people equate themselves with, or identify with, the contents of their thought system. They attach their identity to their beliefs, their values, and their personal version of reality because this is what they *think* they are. This innocent misunderstanding is the most efficient way to feel insecure, because any time this image or belief appears to be threatened, we feel as if *we* are being threatened. We perceive our identity to be validated or invalidated by other people, depending on whether or not they accept our beliefs, values, and ideas so on. Since other people are similarly locked into their personal frames of reference, they will frequently perceive things differently and behave differently than what we expect. This difference leads to feelings of insecurity. The more insecure we feel, the greater our need to defend ourselves by upholding or attempting to prove our image. The more we defend our image, the more we become entrenched in the frame of reference that produced the image in the first place. One of the ironies of life is that human beings become attached to the content of their individualized thought system, even though that attachment results in misunderstandings, low self-esteem conflicts, and emotional stagnation.

WHAT IS EGO?

Ego is simply an idea, a pattern of thought that we have developed of who we are and what we have to do to prove ourselves to the world. This idea or image comes with standards of behavior or performance that we believe must be met before we can feel good about ourselves. In lower levels of understanding, defending or supporting this ego becomes the most important thing in the world. We will go to great lengths to keep our view of life, our separate reality, intact. The ego, or self, is a *concept* created out of thought. In actuality, ego is neither an entity nor a force. It has no existence outside of thinking.

Ego and insecurity are two sides of the same coin. They are interconnected and interrelated to the point where you cannot have one without the other. In order to realize how we create our personal and interpersonal problems, we must begin to grasp the dual role of ego and insecurity. Since ego is a concept derived from the thought system, it is susceptible to invalidation by anything that appears to differ with or in any way contradict its existence. Ego exists as a highly personalized state of mind. It is a limited, circular frame of reference. Therefore, the ego perspective is incapable of seeing beyond itself to a larger picture. As a separate reality, this ego state is therefore incapable of explaining, proving, or changing its own existence. Our image of self-importance gets lost in the content and details of our own thinking, because it is part of that thinking. A most important thing to keep in mind is that this egotistic experience exists only because of a human being's ability to think insecure thoughts and not be conscious of where those thoughts are originating. Ego exists because a human being can think (and believe) that he or she is incomplete, unworthy, unlovable, or incompetent. Unknowingly, that same human being is bringing these thoughts to life through that very ability to think.

EGO AND CHANGE

Ego and insecurity are functionally related to protect and defend against change. It is insecurity that makes it seem important that we protect our thought system or our particular set of beliefs. Why? Because the ego is derived from the thought system and all human beings have been taught to be insecure. We have all learned fear and it has become an integral part of our thinking process. We are taught to adhere to a particular set of beliefs. We are taught that we must defend these beliefs in order to protect ourselves. When we are in insecure states of mind, with ego in full bloom, we must, at all costs, argue, defend, and attempt to prove whatever it is that we believe. Being so sure that what we think is right, we feel compelled to fight over stored bundles of information. If the state is low enough, we will go so far as to hurt people and feel that we have served the cause of right. Ego, and its counterpart, insecurity, must validate their own existence, they must maintain the status quo. Therefore, ego and change are mutually exclusive.

Ego and insecurity are attributes of lower levels of consciousness where the knowledge of the source of thought, separate realities, and feeling is obscured. Insecurity leads us to identify with our thought system and to try to think our way out of the problems that this system has created while keeping intact the beliefs (including) our identity that are the psychological source for these problems. Obviously, this is impossible. However, in lower levels of consciousness, this is precisely what we attempt to do.

As we gain more understanding of the role of thought, we move into higher states of mind, we tap into our common sense and wisdom and are able to see life from a higher, truer perspective, a perspective that is free from biased thinking. In higher levels of consciousness we see the relativity of our "identity" as simply stored information. We realize that we are something more profound than what we think about and we recognize that people live in separate realities, whether or not they realize it. In higher levels, our stored information is neutralized because we are able to see its relativity from a more impersonal vantage point. In higher levels, we experience a clearer state of mind where our stored information does not interfere with our innate feelings of well-being. Past experiences, positive or negative, are recognized as only previous events which are carried through time in a form called memory. In contrast, lower levels of consciousness are accompanied by a level of insecurity that makes our memory of the past seem critically important. In lower states, our perspective is narrow and myopic and we live confine ourselves to realities that are contaminated by thoughts from the past. In these states of mind, we are imprisoned in the content of our own thinking with no notion whatsoever of our own role in creating (or re-creating) that content in the present.

The idea that human beings need an ego to live, to be mentally healthy, to succeed in life, or to know who we are, is completely false. Since our egos are nothing more than conditioned thinking, the opposite is true. The ego is an illusion that requires a thinking human being to seemingly exist. The truth of the matter is that human beings do not even have egos. People only have an ego because they *think* they do. We can only succeed and know who we are when we soften our need to prove and/or improve our own thought-created self. Once we stop catering to our own insecurity and the ego that is attached to it, we begin to live our lives outside of the ordinary ups and downs of life. We begin to live outside the realm of misunderstandings, expectations, beliefs, and images. We move away from conflicts and can see the fallacy of using our conditioned thoughts to tell us how to "cope" with life, or "work things out." An individual living outside the realm of ego, outside the realm of his or her personal insecurity will not be afraid of or reactive to another person's beliefs, opinions, or judgments, for they will no longer be seen as a threat or as something to fear.

In higher states of consciousness, our personal ego vanishes and we are able to see the fact of other people's separate realities without judgment or fear. Thus we are able to live our lives with more kindness and compassion. With a reduction in our attachment to ego, we are relatively free from personal needs. We are living at a level of fulfillment and satisfaction in life at which we don't feel a need to make unreasonable demands on other people. We don't go through life demanding that other people make us happy (we are already happy) or bend to our beliefs about the way things should be.

This is not to say that when we lose what we think is our ego we are passive, unmotivated and have no standards. In fact, the opposite is true. Free from the restricting beliefs of who we think we are, we become stronger, more interested in life, more motivated and productive. If anything, our standards get higher. But instead of using negativity as a way of achieving our goals, we work for the common good by using our mental health to achieve what we want with peaceful methods. This understanding has helped parents, teachers, managers, and supervisors achieve the results that they wanted without resorting to manipulation and control tactics. Dropping personal ego allows us to see alternatives and options that were invisible to us when we were wrapped up in insecure thought to the exclusion of all else.

For example, Carol often felt a great deal of insecurity in her role as an elementary school teacher. When students misbehaved or failed to do their assignments, Carol would take this behavior personally and feel that the students were threatening her authority and her competence as a teacher. Carol's typical response to this behavior was to overreact and attempt to impose a rigid authority on her students. Carol's insecurity would actually escalate a normal classroom dilemma into something unpleasant and unproductive. Carol sought help when she became increasingly irritated and hostile toward one particular youngster who was consistently misbehaving and having learning problems. Ironically, one of the things that Carol had to learn to do in therapy was to be a student again. She learned about thought and how people unknowingly become trapped in the insecurity generated from having to prove themselves to others. She became less attached to her image of self-importance, her ego. She stopped thinking so much about herself and dropped her insecure thinking patterns. This allowed her to regain the positive feelings that had prompted her to become a teacher in the first place. Gradually, she began to notice that she no longer took this particular student's (or any other student's) behavior personally. Her new understanding allowed her to see that this youngster's behavior, like her own behavior in the past, was a product of his insecurity. She recognized that much of his misbehavior was an innocent reaction to the manner in which she tried to change his behavior. This new perspective allowed Carol to begin to help this student instead of punishing him for being insecure. Carol was able, over the next few months, to help this student drop his insecurity and begin to enjoy learning. One of the things that was most beneficial for Carol, was her realization that her best teaching occurred when she was simply relaxed, being herself, and not trying to maintain her image of "teacher."

Dropping our attachment to ego and insecurity always allows us to see a situation with more clarity. Without insecurity to obscure our vision, we are able to live with and enjoy people who live in realities that are different from our own. This is helpful because every other person on the face of the earth lives in a reality that is separate from our own. Living outside of the boundaries of our own thought system, free of our image of self-importance, we experience a sense of contentment that is not dependent on the rest of the world conforming to our beliefs. A person living outside of his ego would call himself an ordinary person. Yet these "ordinary" people appear to be extraordinary to the people around them, because people without ego pressures are the people who get the job done easily, with pleasure, creativity, and without stress.

When a human being drops insecure thought and moves out of a lower level of consciousness into a higher state of mind, ego is neutralized. When this happens, a person begins to experience the natural feeling of self-esteem. Self-esteem is a feeling of appreciation for what we are rather than who we are or what we are doing. It is a feeling of gratitude just to be alive. It is a feeling without fear, without insecurity. Self-esteem has no drive to prove itself. It is a feeling of enjoying our accomplishments while looking forward to new challenges and adventures. Self-esteem is the opposite of ego. It is a healthy feeling that produces positive results. Ego, on the other hand, is a negative feeling of a doubtful self that must be continually supported, boosted, validated, and defended. Thus ego produces insecurity and stress.

Each person has had the experience of living outside of their conditioned thinking. We have all had times when life seems to flow smoothly. When things come up that need our attention, we take care of them without the strain of excessive personal investment. We find that we enjoy ordinary activities, such as driving to work or sitting on the lawn watching the children at play. Without having to maintain or manage our ego, we are able to relax and enjoy whatever is happening at the moment. We take pleasure in the simple things of life and find ourselves surrounded with quiet beauty. Without ego and insecurity we live in states of consciousness where insights, common sense, and wisdom are available to help guide us through life. The times when people feel the happiest, are the times when they think least about themselves!

Many of today's therapies attempt to help people by building up their ego strengths. The underlying premise is that a strong ego helps the person cope better with an inherently stressful life. However, when we really begin to understand what the ego is, we realize that attempting to help someone psychologically by building up their ego is tantamount to throwing a cinder block to someone who is drowning. The result, invariably, is more conflict and misunderstanding.

RECOGNIZING EGO

Because the illusion of the ego is based on insecurity, it thrives on conflict. In fact, the absence of conflict is a threat to ego. This is because if there is no conflict, there is no reason for the ego to exist. In the absence of conflict, there is nothing to prove, figure out, fight for, or deal with, so the ego has no arena in which to prove itself. Ego, expressed through thoughts of insecurity, is the source of the negativity that a human being feels. Since ego is always accompanied by a negative feeling, we can recognize an unpleasant feeling as a sign that we're in an egocentric state of mind. Any negative feeling is a signal that people, to some degree, are invested or identified with their thought system. This identification produces such feelings as fear, anger, hostility, mistrust, suspicion, possessiveness, or jealousy. When people are caught up in these feelings without knowing that these emotions are a by-product of thinking, it may appear that these feelings are primarily the result of some external situation or event. The truth of the matter is that any negative feeling that we have is psychological feedback. Thus, if we hate someone, we may feel that that person deserves it but overlook the fact that we are the one stuck with the hateful feelings.

The actual role of feelings is simply to let us know our level, whether high or low, of psychological functioning. People who do not realize this basic fact use their negative feelings to justify and support their self-created reality. People caught up in the lower consciousness states of ego and insecurity do not use their own negative feelings as the clue to help them realize what they are doing to themselves through thought. Rather, these people use negative feelings to further justify, support, and boost their separate realities. Because ego is an illusion based in thought, it must be continually recreated in thinking itself in order to maintain its existence.

THE EGO WITHIN FIELDS OF STUDY

As will be discussed in greater detail in Chapter 11, the condition of ego is not limited to individuals, but also exists and operates in an identical manner in groups or organizations of people. Groups of people quite often identify themselves with their endeavors. This is evident if we consider that any group or field of people represents a collectively accepted bundle of ideas, concepts, beliefs, and values, which are themselves systems of thought. All frames of reference, whether individual, cultural, or group, operate in the same way. Thus, except for the prevailing level of wisdom of its units, any group of people will become lost in a self-serving image of its own making, and it will do this even to its own eventual disadvantage.

The mental health field as a whole must recognize this phenomenon if it is to evolve beyond the current boundaries of its present thought. The field must see that it is not any of the theories with which it is presently associated. The field of mental health is greater than any of its products. In order for the field to advance, we must be willing to take an objective look at ourselves with the same degree of honesty and directness that we ask of those people who turn to us for help. When we take an honest look, it will be apparent that we must break through our own image, our own barriers of thought. In order to grasp new insights we must be willing to suspend our presently accepted thoughts about human behavior.

The most basic problem that any field faces in its evolution is its own current system of thinking. This is because any system of thought will be an internally consistent and self-validating reality. What this means is that the field operates on, and identifies with, a specific framework of beliefs. Accordingly, that field's experience, research, models, and techniques will serve to maintain the consistency of those beliefs. At a given level of understanding, a field will give certain predictable meaning to events, relationships, and situations that are observed. If the field remains at the same level of understanding, it would continue to reexperience the same patterns again and again in various detailed forms. Tied to its own thought system, the field of psychology has not realized that it is the present level of understanding that prevents it from recognizing anything beyond its theories. Psychology as a field will not evolve to another level of understanding until it breaks through its own ego and lets go of its current level of thinking.

It is initially difficult for an individual or a field of study to drop its ego, take a step into the unknown, and allow change to occur. Yet the rewards from having the courage to take this step are tremendous. Each time we honestly see what we are doing at one level of consciousness and drop our attachment to that level, we advance to a new level. Each higher level is accompanied by new insights, new knowledge, and more mental health. Thus, as those in the field evolve in their understanding of thought, they will themselves become models of mental health.

CHAPTER SEVEN

Wisdom, Insight, and Psychological Change

Throughout time, humanity has sought to understand the words of the enlightened people of this world who have tried to improve the human condition. People have searched for the magic ingredient that would help them change conditions of mental disturbance and interpersonal conflict to conditions of mental health and cooperation. Such knowledge would be known by its results, but a look at human social and psychological conditions suggests that the desired change has come grudgingly over thousands of years and is microscopic. When progress in the human condition is compared to technological advancement, we find that our understanding of human psychological behavior has grown at a snail's pace. The words of the wise, which we revere, profess, and often quote, have remained words and have never become reality for most people. Why? What is missing?

The factor that has been missing in humanity's understanding has been the psychological recognition that perceptions, feelings, and behaviors are shaped by thoughts. As we have noted in earlier chapters, people have tried to understand life from the perspective of whatever thought system they acquired during their life. For this reason, it has been next to impossible for people to profit from what those who have achieved a deeper understanding of life have tried to convey. The reason for this is simple. At higher levels of consciousness, people see life in a simpler, less complex, and, in essence, more truthful way. These individuals, in touch with common sense, have a clearer picture of life. Now, someone who is in a different reality, one that is at a lower level of understanding, relatively devoid of common sense, would see the actions of the other as being wiser. This is why at many points in history, people with an extraordinary degree of common sense, relative to their contemporaries, have been referred to as being "wise." These wise men or women have been thought to possess something called "wisdom." So what is wisdom?

WISDOM AND MENTAL HEALTH

Wisdom is a level of intelligence, innate in every human being, which is deeper and more comprehensive than what we associate with an IQ score. Wisdom exists outside of individualized frames of reference, which is why it has not been more readily realized by a humanity that is wedded to fixed patterns of thinking and perceptions of reality. When wisdom is realized by an individual, it frees him from his own fixed views of life and guides that person toward the attainment of self-esteem, peace of mind, happiness, creativity, and productivity. In other words, wisdom shows the individual how to live in the state of mental health.

What we have begun to realize in the course of our studies is that wisdom is synonymous with understanding thought, reality, emotions, and levels of consciousness. Thus, when we read accounts of truly wise people, it becomes apparent that they were mentally healthy in a way that was so far beyond the realm of what was normal in their time, that their contemporaries (at varying levels of consciousness) either viewed them as a blessing or as a threat. In either case, people have always found it very difficult to listen to what the wise have said about how life works.

What we are saying is simply this: These wise people that we have revered were people who broke the barrier of humanity's thought-created reality and realized that humanity's problems were indeed thought-created. Wisdom, in essence, is mental health, and mental health, as we have noted, is a state of mind in which the human being understands the psychological principles of human reality. This is why the "wise," irrespective of culture, warned people about the perils of judging what is "out there." They were warning us about judging our own perceptions or misperceptions. They told people to look *within* for wisdom, noting that it did not exist in the realm of what mankind perceives to be real. And all pointed toward the feeling of love and goodwill as the route to a better reality.

WISDOM AND INSIGHT

The realization of wisdom occurs in a very natural and sponta- neous manner which is sometimes dramatic, but more frequently subtle. Sometimes wisdom is realized through an insight that breaks into our thought like a light being turned on in a dark room; other times wisdom appears quietly, as though a new thought crept silently into our awareness without our suspecting its importance at first, and later we cannot recall how it came. It was simply there, complete, obvious, relevant. When wisdom is realized, it reveals the unknown. It may show us a missing piece or an appropriate answer that seems so simple and obvious that we wonder how we could not see it before. The conscious state that provides the perspective to see obvious, positive answers is what we are calling common sense.

Everyone has had flashes of wisdom but some people have man- ifested it more consistently than others. The experience and expression of wisdom has been a haphazard affair because until now no one has understood this intelligence as a psychological factor. Most people have placed wisdom beyond the reach of their lives. Yet there are undeniable clues that wisdom is already within each human being. For example who could deny that a person in a mentally healthy state of mind acts wiser than when that person is in a lower state of mind. Who could deny that a person behaves wiser in a good mood than in a bad mood?

The beginning of wisdom is the realization that the human being has the ability to think. Everyone would agree of course, that human beings think. However, very few people realize that ability as a creative, voluntary function. People experience their ability to think as a passive review of data that is being imposed upon them. To see that the human mind has the ability to create thoughts and project them into forms that we call experience, is to understand that we can consciously nurture our mental health. Wisdom reveals to the individual that through the ability to think, that individual is creating the separate reality that becomes his life. Such understanding allows the individual to see beyond his personal frame of reference and find the common sense answers to life's questions.

THE EXPERIENCE OF INSIGHT

Wisdom cannot be realized through mental struggle or the intellectual process of trying to figure out our problems. The reason that wisdom is not more frequently recognized is that human beings have traditionally idolized intellectual and analytical reasoning, and wisdom does not come from these thought patterns. We have missed wisdom because we have learned to think in terms of our problems, to be "realistic," and to sort through our stored information for the answers that we seek. We have literally been looking for our answers in the wrong place without knowing it. All that we can think about is what is programmed into our biological computer.

This is not to say that our thought system has no use. Of course it does. As we have repeatedly noted, it is the perfect tool for accessing useful memory so that we don't forget our language or how to get to work, our telephone number or where to put the dishes when we take them out of the dishwasher. In other words, our thought system is our biological computer and it should be used to help us out in the same way that we utilize a personal computer. We would not consult our personal computer to tell us what to do when our teenager is taking drugs or how to make up with our sweetheart. This would be an obvious misuse of the computer. In the same way, we learn not to use our thought system for things that are beyond its capabilities.

When we realize knowledge that is beyond the software of our biological computer, this is called the experience of insight. Once we experience insight, we realize our capability to drop habits of anxiety, fear, insecurity, and worry. Once we do this we start to live in a more positive feeling level. This feeling level allows us to see things with clarity and objectivity. We regain our self-esteem and our sense of humor and move naturally into states of mind where we feel increased joy and appreciation for the simple things in life. Enjoying what we have opens us to beauty and possibilities that were unseen before. Gratitude for what we have increases the positive feelings which lead us deeper into states of mind where wisdom and insight are found.

Wisdom comes through insight, which is the act of seeing within ourselves and recognizing how our psychological functioning works. Wisdom is not to be found in information. Neither can wisdom depend on an idea, concept, theory, opinion, or belief because all of these things vary from individual to individual, theorist to theorist, profession to profession, culture to culture. Wisdom is not derived from the content of a frame of reference. Rather, the first step toward true wisdom involves the realization that other realities exist. Wisdom is the knowledge that beliefs and ideas are merely thoughts that can lock people into certain perceptions, feelings, and behaviors. Wisdom is a higher vantage point that is unobstructed by personal beliefs, attitudes, opinions, and biases. Wisdom is the intelligence of consciousness that exists before the creation of thought content. For this reason, wisdom cannot be taught to one person by another. It must be realized through the experience of insight. It is difficult, if not impossible, for one person to communicate insight to another person, because wisdom is not a thinking process. Wisdom is the spontaneous appearance of knowledge.

To understand wisdom, we can look at the two distinct approaches that people take in putting a jigsaw puzzle together. The more insecurity we have about completing the puzzle, the more we focus on the separate pieces of the puzzle and the more difficulty we have in putting the pieces together. When we lose sight of the overall picture we get lost in the parts. It is a simple case of not being able to see the forest for the trees. However, the moment that we relax and begin to enjoy the puzzle, the easier it becomes to see what pieces are out of place. As we begin to work, not so much with the separate pieces, but with the whole picture, our view becomes broader, more objective. As we find more missing pieces, the picture becomes more complete, and we are able to see each piece in relation to the whole picture. In states of wisdom, we have an objective clarity that guides us to see a bigger picture rather than to spend our time trying to figure out each piece. In an analogous way, wisdom helps us keep the details of life in perspective.

We ask our computer to do an impossible task when we ask it to tell us the meaning of life. The moment we see the futility of trying to use our thought system in this way, we cease to struggle, we relax, and our wisdom and common sense emerge naturally. We begin to know the experience of insight. It is insight that helps us realize facts about the workings of our thought systems, so we are able to see beyond our existing frames of reference. Insights show us how the conditioning process works. They show us what a thought is and what a belief is so that we are no longer at the mercy of perceptions resulting from beliefs and conditional thinking. Insights show us how we move from one belief system to another or, more to the point, how we move from one reality to another. Insights, similar to the ones that we used to learn a language when we were babies, show us the simplicity of life. Insights are a function of a higher level of consciousness, a level where we are guided by positive feeling and effortless knowing that allows us to live the lives that we want to have and to be successful and happy, regardless of the beliefs, opinions, or biases of the people around us.

By definition, an insight must be fresh, useful, and positive. An insight will never produce negativity or fear. Negativity is a sign that a person is responding to negative conditioning. Conditioning and insight are mutually exclusive and it is important to a person's mental health to be able to distinguish one from the other. A true insight will always show a better, more positive understanding than was previously seen. A true insight is a highlight, a purely pleasurable experience that increases our feelings of well-being and self-esteem. If a negative thought intrudes upon our awareness, bringing with it a feeling of repulsion, dread or fear, the negative feelings immediately tell us that we have tapped into conditioning from the past and are going in the opposite direction of our mental health.

A perfect example of an insight occurred in 1928. For nearly a century, researchers had been desperately searching for something that would kill the various kinds of bacteria that cause deadly infections. The scientific search for such a compound involved, among other things, growing colonies of the types of bacteria that were known to be pathogenic. One fateful day, while inspecting the cultures of bacteria growing in petri dishes, the director of a lab noticed that one of his dishes had been contaminated. Earlier that week he had opened that dish to extract some of the bacteria. When he did, some stray mold must have contaminated the bacterial colony. This was not an uncommon occurrence; it happened in all laboratories and all that a researcher could do was to contain his anger and frustration, discard the contaminated colony, and begin all over again. This particular researcher had experienced this same situation many times in his career. On this occasion, however, before discarding the dish as he was accustomed to doing, he held it up to the light and took another look at the green mold that had ruined his experiment. To his astonishment, he noted that for a considerable distance around the mold, the bacterial colony was undergoing lysis—something was dissolving the bacteria! The researcher, of course, was Alexander Fleming and the mold was penicillin. What had "ruined" this man's research was the answer he was seeking. One can only be grateful that on this one occasion, a human being took one look beyond his disappointment. So what began as a disaster, from the point of view of Fleming's conditioned thinking, ended up being one of the greatest scientific discoveries of the century.

While the above example shows how an insight can result in a breakthrough in the physical health of humanity, an insight can also assist an individual in attaining more mental health in everyday life, by shedding new light on his or her problems.

A person's conditioning might lead her to react negatively in a certain situation. Take, for example, a client named Ann, a teacher who had come to therapy because of job-related stress. On her way to therapy one day, Ann was caught in a rush-hour traffic jam. As usual, she began to think the negative thoughts that were so familiar to her. She became tense, angry, and hostile toward other drivers. In her frustration, she began to honk her horn and make insulting comments to other drivers. All of a sudden, one of the drivers, a young man in the car next to hers, looked at her and said, "Lady, take it easy." Ann's initial reaction was to become enraged, but then she remembered where she was going. She realized she was late for a session where she hoped to find some peace of mind. Ann very quickly recognized that what she had been told by her therapist was not only applicable to the classroom, but also to her reality in her car. With this realization, Ann sat back, put some good music on her cassette player, and dropped all her thoughts of needing to hurry. She realized that if she was going to arrive late, she might as well arrive with her well-being intact. This was a turning point for Ann, who for the first time in her life began to see the difference between habit and insight. (As it turned out, Ann arrived 20 minutes late, but had to wait another 20 minutes, as her therapist was also stuck in traffic!)

The individual who experiences such an insight enters into a more positive reality than the one she lived in prior to the insight. What makes the examples of Alexander Fleming and Ann noteworthy is that both exemplify insight. So whether one achieves indirect relief through an insight of how to stop an infection or gains direct relief by realizing that one is inflicting oneself with negative thinking, the end result is the same: A new reality is found.

Adding the dimension of wisdom and insight to psychology is analogous to adding a third dimension to a two-dimensional geometry. It is a shift to a larger, more encompassing, more objective frame of reference. This broader frame of reference includes what was there before, and more. It gives a new meaning and significance to what was previously experienced.

PSYCHOLOGICAL FRAMES OF REFERENCE AND CHANGE

Before wisdom is realized, people live in their beliefs. A belief system is a psychological frame of reference that limits and distorts our vision of life, and leads to habitual behaviors. It is possible to make a horizontal shift within a frame of reference, which simply means moving from one belief system to another. A person's reality can be changed, to a new *conditioned* reality. This, of course, will change the pattern of behavior. It must be emphasized that this change is not to a new level of understanding reality, but is a shift at the same level to a different pattern. The process by which an individual is conditioned to a new set of beliefs without being aware of it is called a "conversion process." Such conversion processes do not involve any real change in the level of understanding, but are simply ways in which individuals transfer their insecurities from one thought pattern or set of beliefs to another.

If we look at conversion or reconditioning processes, we find that these processes always involve certain "commitment mechanisms" that ensure that people adhere to and identify with a particular ideology or belief system. In order to be converted to certain beliefs, people are subjected to initiations that involve highlighting their fears and inducing embarrassment, emotional catharsis, and emotional or physical exhaustion. These techniques are used to make people feel that they cannot have well-being or self-esteem without belonging to the group. These procedures foster a we–they mentality that excludes the rest of the world from their group. This intensifies the pressure to conform to the group's behavioral, moral, and attitudinal norms, or to face the insecurity of being rejected from the group. Conversions can never involve a shift to a higher level of understanding because this would obviate people attaching their well-being or security to a belief system.

On the other hand, there is another order of change, one that does not merely involve substituting one belief for another. This is the kind of shift that is involved in realizing wisdom or common sense. The shift to a psychological frame of reference of wisdom involves no conversion processing or reconditioning. This is a vertical shift that involves having an insight or realization about the existence and nature of the frames of reference of conditioned beliefs. When people have this realization, they move to a higher level or perspective where they are able to live outside of their conditioning. There is no need for individuals at these higher levels to attach themselves to any particular group, ideology, or movement, as they have little need to base their self-esteem or well being on anything outside of themselves.

Moving from the psychological frame of reference created by a thought system to the frame of reference of wisdom is not a parallel movement across the same level, but a vertical transfer to a new level. This vertical shift can be compared to a change in understanding that happens in elementary school. In first grade, the teacher wanted us to learn the principle of addition. Since a principle cannot be articulated, the teacher presented us with example after example to show the result of the principle. At first, not knowing the principle of addition, we had no choice but to practice, drill, and memorize examples that were presented to us by the teacher. But at some point, we had an insight that showed us the comprehensive picture behind all the examples that the teacher had presented. From that moment on, we were able to add an endless variety of numbers, not from practice, but from a realization of the logical relationships involved in the problem. With this realization, we moved from a conditioned frame of reference to the larger, unconditioned frame of reference.

Learning the principle of addition is a recapitulation of learning to live life successfully. We are all taught to try to be loving, grateful, courteous, patient, fair, just, forgiving, understanding, and respectful of others. But how many people are successful at arriving at these correct answers when faced with the problems that they encounter in the course of their life? Very few. The reason for this is that these qualities are not techniques or causes, they are effects. They are the effects of living at a level of consciousness where one sees that every human being is acting according to the limits of his or her understanding. It is obvious that at any given moment, it is impossible for someone to be nonjudgmental, patient, loving, or forgiving if their level of consciousness is such that the reality they are feeling and perceiving is threatening, hurtful, harmful, or hostile. What few people realize is that all the positive attributes that people try so hard to live up to, as well as all those negative attributes which we try to suppress, are attributes of our level of consciousness rather than our beliefs. So the answer lies in raising one's level of consciousness above the level where we are constantly trying to be good by fighting off our negative desires. Figure 5 graphically depicts how our level of consciousness typically manifests itself. The upper half of this diagram denotes levels of consciousness where people see realities that are positive and thus elicit from them what most of us consider virtues, while the lower half denotes levels of consciousness where the realities that are perceived are more negative in nature and thus elicit all of humanity's shortcomings.

Insights are one of the natural outcomes of living in an unconditioned frame of reference. These insights give us working knowledge of the principles of thought, separate realities, levels of consciousness, and the role of feelings. As people advance through levels of consciousness, they learn to move through realities. True responsibility becomes a fact as individuals realize that the world is not what is really affecting them, but that they are, in fact, shaping their own experience in life through their own thinking.

Wisdom, Insight, and Psychological Change

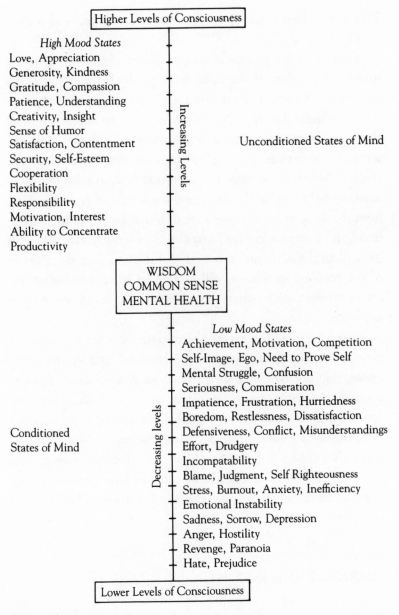

Figure 5

The Characteristics of Conditioned and Unconditioned Frames of Reference

This is the beginning of wisdom, common sense, and mental health.

Wisdom, by the process of insight, reveals the futility of trying to solve a problem at the same level at which the problem was created by thought and perceived as reality. When this is recognized, an individual realizes that any method, technique, or ritual that comes out of thinking at a lower level of consciousness only serves to perpetuate the level of consciousness at which it was created. When we attempt to use information to solve our problems, we fail to realize the deeper principle that all problems result from thinking in an insecure state of mind. In problematic situations, the solutions involve using common sense to take whatever immediate measures are indicated and then to drop the thought of the problem so that we will be free to move into higher levels of consciousness where an obvious, simple answer will be apparent.

We have all had the experience of trying to solve a problem by mental struggle. No matter how hard or how long we think, the answer will not come. However, once we give up trying to think about it and relax, watch television, or take a walk, the answer appears spontaneously in our thoughts. Reports of major scientific breakthroughs are filled with accounts of scientists who exhausted themselves trying to figure out a complex problem, gave up, and put their minds on something else, only to have the solution appear suddenly and effortlessly. This is an example of how the process of insight works.

LEARNING AND INSIGHT

Insights are a natural part of every human being's experience in life. As babies and young children, we learned to walk and talk, tie our shoes, and climb stairs all without conscious effort. Learning was effortless and pleasurable because we were experiencing life from within, with nothing in the way of learning and enjoyment. We did not think about or judge these experiences; thus we were unaware of the fact that we were "learning" anything. We were simply enjoying life. However, as we developed our thought system, we became so identified with it that we forgot about the insight experience and began to experience life from the perspective of other people's beliefs and expectations. Then the process of learning became attached to our thinking process, and we began to run into difficulties.

This is why children can learn languages with ease but for most adults it is a struggle. The trouble is that adults try to learn from the perspective of the language they already know. Their inability to let go of one to experience another impedes their learning. We have seen six-year-olds, who had used their natural process of insight to become fluent in two languages, suddenly have a "learning disability" in school after being conditioned by insecure thought. These "learning-disabled" students became fluent in two languages without teachers, without programmed learning, without memorization or drill. Learning by insight, mastery of two languages was part of their play. But in the classroom, the function of insight is replaced by the memorization and utilization of information. When this happens, spontaneous learning is impeded by compulsive thinking. We take the pleasure out of learning and make it difficult. From this point on, experiencing life from within—using insight—rather than from the thought system becomes the exception to the rule.

It takes some degree of courage to look at what we believe and to realize that much of what we believe to be true about how human beings function is based on misperceptions that have been handed down to us. But this realization must happen before we are willing to let go of the old to make way for something new. We have to be willing to do this before we can move into a larger realm of knowing that is not dependent on the stored information in our biological computer. Once we realize that there is more to life than what we think, our thought process softens, we become emotionally relaxed, and we discover new, positive feelings that indicate that we are in a state of mental health. These positive feelings bring us not only creativity, satisfaction, and happiness, but also a source of knowledge.

Wisdom has nothing to do with IQ scores or station in life. It has nothing to do with information or the ability to develop sophisticated or complex technology. In fact, many of our mental problems are a direct result of not being able to understand our own information and technologies. The deeper knowledge which we refer to as wisdom is not a thinking process. People who idolize their fixed forms of thinking will have difficulty accessing wisdom because thinking, and the insecurity that this thinking produces, is what actually obscures or denies the view within. When we return to the state of innocence of thought that we had as children, we will learn effortlessly, as we did then, all that is necessary for us to have happy, mentally healthy, and successful lives.

To date, very few individuals have even come close to understanding the words of the wise because the principle or essence of what the wise were trying to convey has been hidden by the separate reality of conditioned associations to the language they used—each using whatever words and terms were common to their culture. People have not been able to hear past language or culture. The link that has been missing is the psychological knowledge of thought, separate realities, levels of consciousness, and emotions. This knowledge is the necessary ingredient that begins to decipher the stories, parables, and statements of the wise. It allows the individual to listen beyond the cultural relativity of language to hear the universal wisdom behind the words. The beauty of wisdom, or true mental health, is that when any degree of wisdom is realized, one's level of sanity increases and one can never be as psychologically lost as before. Even more beautiful is the realization that no matter how wise one becomes, there is always more.

CHAPTER EIGHT

The Process
of Therapy:
Guiding Clients
to Mental
Health

A true shift in understanding through which an individual evolves to a higher level of mental health is quite different from what we would call a conversion process, in which an individual is conditioned to a new set of beliefs without being aware of what conditioning is or even that conditioning is occurring. Such conversion processes do not involve any real change in levels of understanding; they are simply a shift from one belief system to another at the same level of consciousness.

Rather than helping clients make a horizontal shift from one belief to another at the same level of consciousness, we as therapists want to assist them to make a vertical shift to a higher level of consciousness where they understand the nature of belief systems. We want to help clients shift to higher perspectives where they will see possibilities, solutions, and opportunities that they could not see at lower levels of consciousness. We want clients to shift to a higher level where they will experience greater degrees of well-being, happiness, motivation, and self-esteem. These results will occur when people begin to realize (1) that their views of reality are relative and distorted negatively by acquired patterns of thinking; (2) that each individual lives in a separate reality from every other person; (3) that the levels of consciousness have meaning; and (4) that feelings are indicators of a person's level of psychological functioning. Since these principles are impersonal, they can be related to each person's experience regardless of the symptoms of psychological malfunctioning that the person may have.

Working with this approach, therapy sessions become somewhat impersonal in that they involve teaching the client, in a pleasant, practical way, how human beings function psychologically. The sessions are purposely relaxed and enjoyable experiences

127

that put clients at ease help them to achieve a state of mind open to learning. The goal of therapy is a stable increase in the client's understanding. The therapist is not overly interested in the client's malfunctioning, because psychological malfunction is unavoidable in the absence of knowing about thought, reality, feelings, and moods. Rather, therapy based on the principles presented in this book focuses on unfolding a new psychological vantage point. Since this new vantage point is more natural and effortless than the old one, the client also begins to recognize the difference and to move in a new direction.

In most cases, before the client has even realized that a change has happened, he finds himself taking things less seriously, seeing situations from a new point of view that results in their being less gripped by them than previously. The client begins to recognize the fact of conscious states or separate realities occurring in his day-to-day experience.

When a client is in a lower state of consciousness or a low mood, the therapist spends as much time as necessary helping this individual elevate his mood. This enables the client to relax emotionally and to rise out of his negative perspective so that he will be able to listen and see the larger picture that includes his own psychological functioning. Elevating the client's mood is a crucial part of this new therapy because when a person is in a low mood and feeling insecure, that individual will defend his or her reality, regardless of how painful or unpleasant it may be. In these states of mind, a person may argue, even with their therapist, to maintain their version of what is happening. A person in a low level of psychological functioning would rather be right than happy. But once the mood shifts, the client will see the situation differently, even though none of the details of the circumstances have changed.

For example, one of the authors worked as a counselor in a

school setting and was frequently called upon to take a disruptive student out of the classroom. This would mean that a student was in a negative state of mind to the point where he was creating a disturbance. As the counselor walked down the hall with these students, they would be talking nonstop about how the teacher was out to get them, how the other kids were picking on them, how their parents didn't understand them, how the work was too hard, and on and on. If, at this time, the counselor attempted to tell these individuals that things were not as bad as they thought, the students would argue with increased vigor that things were indeed as bad as, if not worse than, they reported. If the counselor tried to talk the students out of their perception while they were in this mood, the students would insist that the counselor didn't understand their situation.

However, this counselor discovered that if she took these individuals to a quiet place, helped them to relax by resting, reading a book, or listening to music (anything but talk about their problem), in a very short period of time the students' states of mind would automatically rise and they would see things differently. In fact, without exception, once students' states of mind had elevated, the counselor would ask them how things looked now. The students consistently replied that they didn't really know what had happened earlier, but that the teacher was really helpful, the other kids were their friends, and their parents were OK, too. People in higher states of mind, regardless of their age or IQ, have common sense and some degree of wisdom, so they are able to see their situations with more objectivity.

When this shift in state occurred, the counselor would take the opportunity to teach these students, in simple terms, something about their own psychological functioning. She would point out that what had happened was called a low mood and that all people have mood changes during the day. She would briefly describe what a mood is and what the world looks like to a person in a low mood. The students, with a fresh memory of that experience, would recognize the fact. The counselor would also talk about higher moods and what they looked like from the inside. This counselor looked for the teachable moment when an individual would be relaxed and interested; then she would present simple facts of psychological functioning that would help that individual in the future. Even a child could understand the logic of mental health.

THE KEY TO RESPONSIBILITY

Unfortunately, helping people feel better is not always seen as direct or simple. The fields of mental health and therapy today still assume that people are prisoners of their personalities, habits, or pasts. Yet from the previous example, we see that people fluctuate in and out of their attachment to these prisons, depending on their level of psychological functioning, or their states of mind. When a therapist does not recognize this fact, he or she will tend to keep clients in their prison cells by validating the notion that the clients have a serious problem that is being caused by something that they cannot control. With an understanding of how thought works in relation to levels of consciousness, a therapist can help a client become free of personality, habits, and pasts. With this freedom comes an increased sense of choice about a direction in life and new wisdom to choose a positive and productive path. In other words, as people become mentally healthy, they become more responsible people. They are able to see that they are responsible for creating their reality and they begin to stop blaming other people, situations, or events for their feelings.

It is only when people begin to understand the working of thought that it becomes fruitful for them to take responsibility for their experience in life. People can't be forced or told to take responsibility when they don't see their role in the creation of their reality. If counselors push people to accept responsibility that they are not ready to accept, they are asking for the impossible. In this situation, the clients will be likely to experience increased blame or guilt, which is the opposite of responsibility and which is opposed to the desired goal of mental health.

This is the reason why the best way to use our wisdom as therapists is to talk impersonally and objectively from our understanding of the principles that we have recognized. If people honestly want to change, they will listen for themselves and begin to recognize the common sense of what the therapist is saying. This recognition will occur more quickly when both therapist and client are in positive states of mind. Clients report to us that they walk away from sessions feeling relieved, more relaxed and hopeful about their situation. They begin to notice nice things happening around them, perhaps even not yet knowing why they are having these nicer feelings. When they get home and their spouses or children get into old patterns of negativity, these clients do not have the same urge to jump in, as they did in the past. They often surprise themselves by responding in new ways to old situations. They are amazed to see how problems that were overwhelming the day before have obvious, more simple solutions, solutions that had not occurred to them previously.

THE ACTIVE INGREDIENTS IN CHANGE

Often, therapy seems like a difficult process for therapists because the clients, who are caught up at the time in personal upset (seeing things through the perceptual filters created by insecurity), want advice and are asking for solutions that make sense to them in the framework of their present view of the problems. Furthermore, many clients believe that it is therapeutic to talk about their problems and reexperience negative feelings as a way to "get them out." They do not realize that the only way to "get out" of these realities is to move to a state of mind where they do not exist. Therefore, the most helpful aspect of any therapeutic relationship is to guide the clients to realizing wisdom. This occurs naturally when the client knows that wisdom is related to a positive feeling state. Then the client will see beyond the limitations of previous experience and perceptions of problems.

As clients begin to relax, quiet down, listen, and feel less insecurity, the urge to analyze specific problems begins to fade. This opens the way for mental health to emerge from within. As this happens, clients will begin to gain a broader knowledge about the sources of problems and how to live in more secure feeling states. They will readily begin to see the common-sense logic of the principles of psychological functioning that the therapist is describing because they are in a frame of mind where these principles are recognizable as fact.

People in low levels of consciousness cannot comprehend understanding or psychological fact. The only substantial proof of these things comes when their level of consciousness rises and they begin to recognize these shifts in reality. These recognitions are what we call insights—when experience changes for the better and individuals see for themselves that it was their changing psychological state that solved the problem and changed their reality. This is the proof that they were looking for, but this proof only comes from looking within. This proof cannot be given to anyone through words. Words are only a direction to greater understanding. Clients move to higher levels of understanding through positive feelings. We all have the capacity for positive change, but this experience comes not through the intellectual processing of information, but through the positive experience of understanding (insight).

True change cannot occur through information alone. It is the deeper, more objective view given by wisdom that puts information in perspective. People often read a book and find it obscure. Later, they pick up the same book and find it to be more understandable. The reader finds things in the book that were not evident in the first reading. What changed? Was it the information on the pages? Of course not. The obvious answer is that the understanding of the person reading the book had changed. The readers who find increased understanding through reading this book can forget the specific information on the pages and use their common sense which has been activated by the information. As we begin to develop wisdom, we become the source of our own understanding rather than a follower of someone else's thinking.

When we as therapists raise our own levels of consciousness to the point where we are able to recognize separate realities, we realize that no one can do anything that does not conform to their individual reality. If, for example, we are at a certain level of insecurity about intimacy in relationships, we will naturally tend to distance ourselves from people. Advice to attempt closeness in our present frame of reference would result in increased insecurity, frustration, or failure. Change becomes possible only when the client shifts to an objective view which reveals that it was his or her frame of reference that maintained the problem. This person can then realize the possibility and capability for new behavior.

Family counselors and marriage therapists who attempt to take people back into the past to find solutions to present problems will find themselves entangled in an endless maze of confusion and conflicting details. Going into the past to find solutions to present problems is not only time-consuming, emotionally wrenching, and complicated, it also simply does not work. Rather, therapists can help people by showing them that their present problems come from their thinking at a certain level of consciousness. This understanding will help people achieve the kind of relationships that they want to have. This change will come from an understanding that frees people from their past.

When people are troubled, they usually become busy sorting through the data they have stored in their frame of reference. People become so busy listening to this recycling of old data that they cannot hear anything new, something that would take them beyond the limits of their present understanding. When a solution to a problem is not immediately forthcoming, a person's level of insecurity rises and the search through old beliefs, theories, and assumptions becomes more compelling.

The answer to the problem is not to be found in the already formed belief system which produced the perception of the problem in the first place. The answer comes when people disengage from their thought systems and lapse into a state of relative well-being. If they remain in this state for any appreciable length of time, they will begin to access whatever degree of common sense exists at that level of consciousness.

The therapist's major aim is to help each client find a deeper, more factual understanding of life through a calmer, more positive frame of mind. Helping a client to relax and feel safe creates in that client a condition of receptiveness. In quieter states of mind, a client has a greater willingness to consider something outside of what is already believed to be true. When clients are secure, their thinking is less activated. They are then able to observe with more clarity what is really going on. They see the variety of thought systems in the world and how they interact to create whatever is happening at the time. In a calmer and more quiet state, they begin to walk through life with positive feelings that are grounded in the stability of wisdom.

When we quiet down and stop interpreting life in a negative way, life becomes easier. When we have gained a deeper understanding about how things actually do work, rather than how we think they should work, life becomes simpler, more enjoyable. When we as therapists begin to see these possibilities for ourselves, we can point our clients in the same direction.

It is only when we stop trying to control life that we can begin to enjoy it. In the feeling of enjoyment, our thoughts, worries, doubts, resentments, and guilt drop away. Every day becomes an adventure of new experiences, insights, and beauty. To describe this experience in words is impossible. It is similar to a television manufacturer trying to demonstrate that his set offers brighter color and a clearer image by showing a picture of his television screen in a commercial on a competitor's TV. The picture that we see cannot be any better than the screen we are viewing.

The way to obtain a better screen, one consisting of increased objectivity, clarity, and common sense, is not through analyzing the details of the picture that we see. Instead, we must change levels so that we see a different picture. We need to see more clearly how our thought systems are projected outward to form the details or picture of our life. As therapists, we guide clients toward this vantage point. From this higher, clearer perspective they can begin to experience the change for themselves. This is the thrust of the therapist's work.

INSECURITY AND THERAPY

When therapists themselves drop insecurity, they can begin to see how insecurity works in their clients. Therapists will see people's insecurities taking various forms, such as overindulgence in working, eating, drinking, smoking, or using drugs. Other people express insecurity by picking fights or becoming depressed or para-noid. The therapists who understand insecurity go directly to the source to show their clients what insecurity is. If we as therapists are insecure ourselves, we cannot do this because we are in the same boat as our clients.

The power of dropping negativity by realizing that insecurity is only a thought is far more effective than any attempt to learn better ways to cope with or understand our problems. The results of these realizations are predictable. If we drop insecurities, we must see things differently; we must move to a new level of consciousness. Without the filters of irrational fears, we do not focus exclusively on our own needs and concerns. We do not worry about what people are doing in relation to us. We see their behavior more objectively—not how it relates to our realities, but what it means to them in their realities.

For example, an attorney dropped out of his profession because he was intimidated by the intelligence and seeming unapproach-ability of other lawyers and judges within the courtroom. He was insecure about his skills and his ability to do his job. Once this man realized that his perceptions were a result of living within the framework of insecure thinking, he was able to disengage from this frame of reference and move to a higher level of psychological functioning where he saw things differently. He was able to return to his profession. He began to realize that many of the lawyers he had idealized for their aggressiveness were insecure themselves. He stopped comparing himself to other people and concentrated on doing his work to the best of his ability. He began to receive positive feedback about the ease and naturalness of his courtroom manner. He found that when he felt secure he was able to stay on the point and not get rattled by other people's tactics. He became an effective lawyer who enjoyed his work. This change occurred naturally when this man realized how his thoughts were creating his negative feelings which, in turn, were creating ineffective behavior. His understanding of his own psychological functioning allowed him to quiet down his negative thoughts so that he could experience the true change that occurs with a shift in the level of consciousness.

USING OUR PERSPECTIVE

It is only when we gain a perspective of the bigger picture beyond the beliefs we are trying to maintain that we realize how everything we are doing, reacting to, and trying to manage is all a product of those same beliefs. We then realize how much effort, negativity, and stress we experience from attempting to maintain that thought system and to clean up the messes created from it.

Rather than helping clients cope with life by giving them techniques or alternative conditioning, therapists want to give clients themselves direct access to a broader perspective, a realization of the underlying principles of how the mind works. This involves looking in a new direction. As therapists, our aim is to teach clients what we know about psychological functioning. It is quite rewarding to see the results as people begin to catch on and recognize their own capacity for mental health and freedom from the problems that have plagued them. The greatest gift we can give those who come to us for help is to assist them in seeing that they are fully capable of living healthy lives and that when they change, the change is due to their own increased understanding and not to any technique or methods of the therapists. Therapy is truly complete when clients realize that psychological change comes from within and they know the direction for continuing to learn more on their own. There is no greater reward for a therapist than to see a client wake up to his or her own potential.

CHAPTER NINE

Therapy: The Direction and Role of the Therapist

People come to therapy looking for help with problems in their life. They want to tell the counselor not only what the problem is but also the reasons they believe (think) the problem exists. The most common tendency is for the client to describe, in detail, the scenario which is seen as the cause of the problem. This tendency is quite understandable. We have all done this at one time or another, in an effort to feel better while caught up in the separate reality of our thought system. This situation is depicted in Figure 6. For this reason, when people seek professional help, they invariably have a whole set of fixed ideas of what they think the problem is and what will or will not provide relief. This set of fixed ideas is what they want to focus on in therapy. Unfortunately, traditional approaches to psychotherapy do just that; they focus on the details of what the client thinks in a low level of consciousness.

The problem with this approach is that people in trouble are trying to explain why they feel bad in the absence of a knowledge of where feelings come from. These people are attempting to explain their perceptions when they have no true understanding of how perceptions are formulated. In short, a client's reality does not include the knowledge of the source of the discomfort, and this lack of understanding is itself the real problem. If the client understood the true cause of the difficulty, he or she would realize the solution to the problem.

Therapy, if it is to be truly helpful, requires that the therapist understand that what is causing that person's problems. The professional with an understanding of these psychological principles will realize that the client's version of reality is simply a product of his or her psychological functioning at a certain level of consciousness. Therefore, the therapist would not focus primarily on the *product* of the functioning but on the *nature* of the

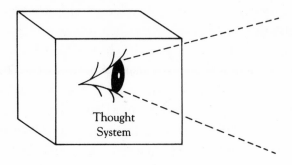

Figure 6.

A psychological state of mind where the individual is confined to the limits of his or her thought system.

functioning itself. In order to accomplish this goal, therapists themselves must be functioning at a level of understanding that is not limited to their conditioned thought system. This level of functioning is depicted in Figure 7. The therapist with this under-standing would know that if the client was in a better or higher state of mind, the particular details of the situation would be per-ceived differently. Instead of focusing on the details produced by a low level of psychological functioning, the therapist would direct the client away from low-mood thinking patterns so that the client's level of consciousness would rise. This is done by teaching the client how patterns of thinking are produced and how they create the emotional environment in which we live. A therapist

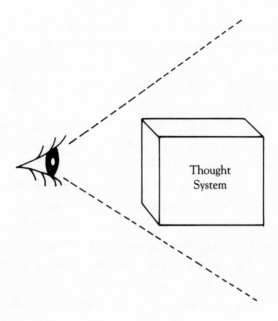

Figure 7.

A psychological state of mind where the individual is not confined to the limits of his or her thought system.

wants to help the client to begin to identify or notice his or her own psychological functioning at work in the present moment. When the client begins to see the role that his or her thinking plays in shaping perception, feelings, and behavior, he or she will gain a larger, much more useful psychological perspective. The vehicle that gives a client this higher perspective is an understanding of psychological principles.

THE PRINCIPLES IN THERAPY

Many people ask how these psychological principles can be used in therapy. The answer is not to be found in a technique or a fixed method to be applied. There are no special words or rituals to be used. The principles of human psychological functioning are applied in therapy through the therapist. The principles work to the degree that the therapist understands and experiences them at a practical level in his or her own life, and of course, the degree to which the client is open to change. The understanding which the therapist possesses will be expressed in his or her manner with the client, personal behavior, and by the atmosphere that is created in the therapy session. The principles can be presented in many different ways. Health and positivity can be expressed and shared in various forms. Likewise, the therapist's conduct will not conform to any set procedure but will always be guided by the level of understanding that the client possesses. The form of the therapy will always point the client toward the principles working behind the scenes of his or her separate reality and will encourage that conscious state of mind in which the client's view becomes clear. Figure 8 illustrates the relative positions of the therapist and the client at the beginning of therapy (position A), and, ideally, where the patient moves, relative to his or her initial frame of reference, by the end of therapy (position B). The goal of the therapist is to assist the client to realize a higher level of consciousness where his or her understanding, thinking, and perceptions of life are freed from the limitations of their conditioned thought system.

A therapist with an understanding of psychological principles will be able to see the separate reality of the client without getting caught in the negative details of that reality. The therapist will look beyond the details of any particular problem to see the way in which psychological functioning was used to produce those details. With this understanding, the counselor will begin to teach the client the principles of psychological functioning as a means of getting the client to recognize his or her role in the creation of reality. In essence, this gives the client a new relationship to re-

144

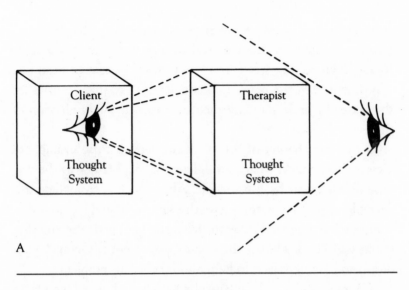

A

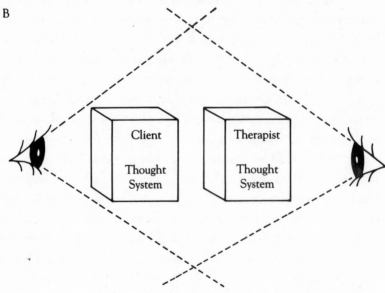

B

Figure 8.

The ideal outcome of the process of therapy

ality. Instead of seeing themselves as victims of a harsh world, clients are able to realize that reality is an extension of thought. Rather than feeling stuck in a reality that appears to be thrust upon them from the outside, clients learn to change realities for the better by understanding their own role in the production of their experience.

In the first chapter of this book, we provided the example of George, along with what four different therapists saw as the way to guide this man back to health. After deciding to include this example, one of the authors gave this same case study to an intern who was learning to do therapy from the perspective of the Psychology of Mind. Here is the intern's assessment of George's condition and her approach to help him get over his problems:

"George appears to be a basically healthy individual who lacks any appreciable knowledge of how a simple bad mood, coupled with thinking, can create a great deal of anguish. The nice thing is that George appears to be a gentle, family-oriented man who seems to have his family's best interest in mind. One of the things that I would tell George is that his thoughts about Laura (his secretary) are quite natural, especially given the state of mind he was in when he had a fight with his wife. The important point I would make would be that there are thoughts that become intensified in low mood states and that it is precisely such thoughts that one learns not to take seriously. This is important because George does not know about levels of consciousness, and so he may be frightened at not being able to understand why he sometimes wants to be an ordinary family man, play his bassoon, and be a father, while at other times he is obsessively attracted to someone like Laura. It would be important for George to understand that his desires will change along with his state of mind. Another thing that I would do is help George realize that his problem really has nothing to do with Ann or the baby they are expecting, or even with Laura. His problem is that George doesn't know that he is thinking himself into a problem or that his feelings come from within himself and not from his secretary, his wife, or his unborn child. Finally, I would help George to appreciate his wife and to look forward to their new baby."

PHYSICIAN, HEAL THYSELF

The most important thing that therapists can do to help clients is to become responsible, effective, and happy people themselves. The old admonition, "Physician, heal thyself," is based on wisdom. If a therapist does not have a happy marriage, how can that person help others to have a happy marriage? If we do not know how to be successful ourselves, we cannot teach others to be successful.

The main therapeutic tool that a therapist has is his or her level of mental health. This level of understanding will be evidenced by the degree of well-being, happiness, and success in the therapist's life. It is the practical understanding of principles that guides the therapy session. This understanding goes far beyond an intellectual grasp of the principles. A realization of principles means that this level of understanding has become a reality in the therapist's own life. Only from a position of mental health can a therapist guide clients to their own mental health.

Some psychotherapists say that the point of therapy is not to make people happy, but to help them become well adjusted. We are told that "well-adjusted" people are the ones who have learned to live with their problems, to "cope" with their situation. It is a regrettable commentary on the field of mental health that this is the best that present-day psychology has to offer people. Are we content to make clients better adapted to being unhappy? This is not what we want. With an understanding of these basic principles of human psychological functioning, the mental health field can show people how to be mentally healthy, happy, successful, and grateful for their lives.

INTELLECTUALIZATION: THE BARRIER TO WISDOM

We are all taught to be proud of our intellectual ability. As mental health professionals, we are encouraged to look for more information and to compare and contrast theories. We may even be able to talk theoretically about the power of beliefs and how our thought systems are related to experience, but as long as what we are saying is limited to the intellectual level, we are missing the point. We are falling short because we are staying at the level of words and ideas and missing the level of experience. Yet all the time we are talking at an intellectual level, the object of our discussion, our psychological process, is occurring right there, even while we are attempting to conceptualize about it. The only way to really know psychological functioning is to experience it firsthand, in action, within ourselves. Intellectualization about psychological functioning is one step removed from understanding. It is the same thing as trying to understand the sexual act by explaining it. It is impossible to explain an experience. To know the experience we must go beyond talking about it, go beyond thinking about it, and have the experience ourselves. Only then will we have an understanding that is deeper than intellectualization.

Firsthand knowledge of psychological principles of human functioning is the only way to gain common sense or wisdom. Common sense or wisdom does exist and it can be realized, but it can only be grasped through an experience of fact. As therapists, we cannot help our clients by offering intellectual explanations in the absence of our own experience. On the other hand, when we have some degree of real understanding ourselves, we can help clients by guiding them toward their own wisdom or common sense so that they can see for themselves what it is.

INSIGHT IN THERAPY

A therapist with common sense learns to rely on understanding rather than on technique. Each time we talk to a client from a level of understanding, the message will be expressed differently. This is a great benefit to the client because a client that is listening will always hear the message with freshness. Insights cannot be planned in advance. All we can do is live in the frame of mind where insights occur and be present when they arrive. If clients have been given hope and treated with kindness and respect, they will have moved closer to the state of mind where they can hear what the therapist is saying. Because therapy is based on the actual understanding of the therapist, counseling will be done without effort, stress, or burnout. A counselor simply tells clients how people work psychologically to manifest either health or mental disorder. It is an ordinary experience to tell another person something that you know. The difficulty comes when we try to help a person while we ourselves feel lost or confused.

Often therapists will ask for specific words to say when a client says such and such. When you are offering common sense rather than a memorized ritual, there is no need for certain words. We cannot possibly know the answer to that question until the time comes, and when the time does comes, an answer is apparent. It will be an answer that is born out of the situation of the moment, not one that was thought up in advance. It will be an answer based on common sense or insight.

An insight is a precious experience that one can never predict. Similarly, the therapist will never be able to predict when a patient will have an insight. Insights are a natural psychological process. They are a simple, ordinary experience to a person in a relaxed state of mind. In other words, an insight is not accompanied by lightning, emotional catharsis, or any other such dramatics that are often portrayed in films. Take, for instance, the case of Olga, a 44-year-old Latin woman with a sixth-grade education, whom we saw after her suicide attempt over a broken love affair. In the midst of her depression, Olga had decided that the best solution to her suffering was to kill herself. She had used a .357 Magnum revolver to shoot herself in the side. The bullet damaged her ureter, colon, rectum, and vagina and went through to her leg, damaging some of the nerves. Olga spent weeks in critical care. When she was finally transferred to a ward, she began to realize what she had done to herself and became severely depressed again; a psychological consultation was requested by her physician.

On the first visit the psychologist found Olga very depressed. She cried, "I can't conceive of living after having done something so stupid." In the gentlest way possible, the therapist told Olga that although he could not disagree with her that her actions were not smart, her mental health was something that could be lost sight of but not lost. He briefly explained to Olga how thought works to shape the reality we see and feel. He related some stories that illustrated how knowing this fact had helped people who had had similar experiences. Later, Olga said, "What you said was so simple that when you left I just knew I would be fine." From these words, the therapist knew that Olga had experienced a very simple insight. From that time on, Olga's response to therapy was dramatic. By the end of two sessions, her depression vanished and she was happy and looking forward to her discharge. Her dramatic positive turnaround puzzled more than a few people, who, at this point, had never seen someone change so rapidly.

Olga was seen weekly in counseling for the next six months, during which she changed physically and mentally. One measure of her understanding came in a story she shared with her therapist several weeks after her discharge from the hospital. It seemed that because her injuries were self-inflicted, there was some question as to whether the medical services she received would be covered by insurance. Therefore, she was required to visit a certain psychiatric clinic. After the interview, the psychiatrist suggested that the psychotherapy she was receiving was dangerous, because she was too happy and not taking her suicide attempt seriously enough. He warned her that problems such as hers tended to recur and required lifelong treatment. What surprised Olga was that despite what the psychiatrist had told her, she knew her happiness was solidly based on an understanding that this man did not have. However, she saw that this man was genuinely concerned and had given her the best advice he had to offer from his level of understanding. Olga thanked this physician for his concern and assured him that she would take his advice under consideration, to which he responded with relief. She ended her story by saying how grateful she was for what she had learned. At her last follow-up visit, five years after discharge, Olga continued to have the greater understanding and peace of mind that began with one psychological insight.

It is a nice, even exhilarating, feeling to know that just by being ourselves at a certain level of understanding and pointing out what we see, we can be helpful to others. We can operate through common sense and insight and help clients learn to do the same. To do this, we don't have to memorize techniques or study methods. All we have to do is develop a certain degree of understanding of the principles of human psychological functioning and become happy, successful, and mentally healthy ourselves. With this understanding, we live in levels of consciousness where wisdom in the form of insight and common sense direct the therapeutic process.

BURNOUT: KEEPING THE THERAPIST SANE

The term *burnout* in the context of the mental health profession refers to the negative mental and/or emotional reactions experienced by therapists as a result of their work. This burnout reaction can be manifested as any one or a combination of symptoms such as feeling sorrow, anxiety, irritability, overreactivity, depression, job dissatisfaction, lowered productivity, and illness. The issue of burnout has never been directly and honestly addressed. In truth, burnout is another word for psychological dysfunctioning. Burnout exists when the therapist is functioning at a similar level of consciousness as the patient. At lower levels, both the patient and the therapist get caught in negative realities and believe that problems are caused by external factors or conditions.

For therapists who do not understand how realities are created, it is easy for them to begin to identify with their clients' problems and emotional distresses. When professionals experience problems themselves, they have the added burden of hiding the fact that they are in need of help. Such therapists may end up in therapy themselves hearing the same basic procedures they have dispensed to others.

COMMISERATION OR COMPASSION?

Claire, a 42-year-old woman, began therapy four weeks after becoming depressed over the breakup of a yearlong relationship.

152

Claire's psychologist, who was also a woman, told Claire that the reason she had never had a stable relationship with a man was because she still had many unresolved problems involving her relationship with her father, dating back to her adolescence. This psychologist had a special feeling for Claire because she saw a great deal of similarities between her own life and that of her patient. During the sessions, both Claire and her therapist shared with each other many painful memories they recalled from their pasts. They frequently cried together, commiserating with each other's pain.

Claire's psychologist was genuinely concerned for Claire and wished to provide her patient with the very best care possible. However, after almost two months of therapy, Claire became so depressed that she attempted suicide by taking an overdose of barbiturates. Luckily, a friend called a rescue team and after several days in a medical intensive-care unit, Claire recovered. After her discharge, Claire was seen by one of the authors. She was very responsive in therapy. Her mood changed after the first session. By the end of the sixth session she felt stable and returned to her job. This therapist was not at the same level of consciousness as his client. He did not get caught up in Claire's negative perception of reality. He remained outside of this reality as he showed Claire how she was creating and maintaining this reality. While he had compassion for Claire's very understandable and very painful situation, he did not validate that situation by commiserating with Claire about the hopelessness of the situation. Rather, he was able to see beyond her reality to give her hope. Although it was recommended that Claire continue therapy for another six months to deepen her newfound understanding, she did not comply. However, in a follow-up two years later, Claire reported that she had not experienced any recurrence of depression or suicidal thoughts.

Most mental health professionals find it difficult to see an alternative to either becoming emotionally embroiled in their clients' problems and "burning out," or becoming emotionally insensitive to other people. This is because from the perspective of the traditional theoretical beliefs that many therapists embrace, there are no alternatives. This situation involving the level of the relationship between the therapist and the client is illustrated in figure 9. This relationship frequently involves stress for therapists as they are viewing the client's problem at the same level of "stuckness" or in as compelling a way as the client. This is due to the fact that the therapist is operating from a thought system at the same level of consciousness as the client. This thought system, which includes the therapist's theoretical orientation, is just as confining and limiting to the therapist as the client's thought system is to the client. A third alternative, however, becomes obvious with the understanding of the principles that have been developed in this book. This alternative involves an understanding of the difference between *commiseration* and *compassion*. When therapists appreciate the common principles underlying human feelings, this understanding enables them to view the client's predicament with compassion, yet from a higher perspective that provides hope instead of commiseration.

The only real way for therapists to avoid stress and burnout is for them to understand how to maintain their own mental health. The principles of maintaining one's well-being are the same for therapists as for clients. In other words, we as therapists must learn for ourselves what happiness and well-being are and we must understand the relationships of these states of consciousness to our experiences. We can only teach what we actually know. This is why a therapist's level of consciousness, and not techniques, directs the therapy. The therapist's level of consciousness is reflected in how well he or she has learned to live a successful, stress-free, and understanding life, including how to be happy in job, rela-

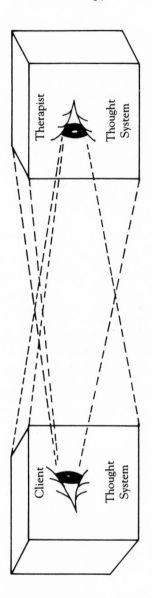

Figure 9.

The situation where both the client and the therapist are caught up in their respective thought systems. For the client, this thought system involves his or her problem whereas the thought system of the therapist involves his or her theoretical views about mental disorders and therapy.

tionships, family, friendships, and other areas of life. When therapists are healthy and happy, their work becomes easier, more enjoyable, and rewarding. Instead of getting caught up in separate realities, they are able to see them with an objectivity that makes them appear to be fascinating learning opportunities for themselves as well as for the client. As we work with our own understanding of psychological principle, our work is enjoyable and we are able to achieve the results that we want.

The therapist who is happy and secure because he or she understands and knows what mental health is, will not commiserate with clients or become frightened or burdened by their realities. A secure therapist will know that there is a way out for the patient and will communicate a genuine feeling of hope and a solid direction for positive change. This therapist has compassion, a feeling of warmth born of understanding. The feeling of compassion sets the stage for a therapeutic atmosphere of openness to positive change.

CHAPTER TEN

The Need for an Advanced Psychology: Toward a Deeper Understanding

From our work over the last 10 years, we have seen that the principles of human psychological functioning that we are presenting in this book do, in fact, provide the basis for precision and consistency for working effectively with people. These principles connect, in a very exact way, consciousness, thought, perceptions, emotions, and behaviors. These principles lead us not only to a deeper understanding of human behavior, but they also provide an understanding of how the field of psychology works. This understanding will enable the field, for the first time in its history, to look within itself to attain validity as a science that is capable of producing consistent results which can be replicated by others in the field.

The field of psychology has depended on the content of its own analytical reasoning to lead it in the direction of progress and results. The problem with such an approach is that any given system of thought, even the system of thought in the field of psychology. Therefore, each formulation from that system will exist as an internally consistent, self-validating reality. That system will operate as a framework of beliefs at a given level of understanding about the subjective reality of those beliefs. Accordingly, as a field, if we assume our psychological beliefs to be absolute, we will continue to perceive reality in a manner that is constrained by those beliefs. That is to say, psychologists make certain interpretations of situations that we experience as a profession and then arrive at certain conclusions that seem to follow from those interpretations. Once an interpretation has been made, that line of thought shapes our perceptions, emotions, and behavior. This is true for individuals, cultures, and fields of study. If a group operates without a conscious understanding about the nature of thought, that group will continue to reexperience the same patterns over and over again in various forms. In other words, without an understanding of the nature of thought, history does indeed repeat itself.

The field of psychology has been living within its own theoretical view. It has been maintaining the status quo by recycling variations of its current thought patterns, without the deeper understanding of the psychological function that is used to create all patterns of thought. The field has lived in its own content, unaware that this content was formulated using a larger, more profound ability, which is the ability to think, or the ability to formulate content. Psychology as a field operates within the limits of a separate, thought-created frame of reference, fascinated and absorbed in the *results* of thinking rather than by the greater *fact* of thinking itself.

PSYCHOLOGY AND SOCIETY

Human beings have an intrinsic desire to understand and to make sense of their world. In an attempt to explain what they see, behavioral scientists often look at events and then designate certain ones as causes and others as effects. In other words, as scientists we observe events and then attempt to explain one event in terms of the other. Associating one event with another in terms of cause and effect can lead to misunderstanding because, in fact, both are already thought-related perceptions. When we overlook this fact, we mistakenly link two things together, which, in fact, have no cause-and-effect relationship. When this occurs, we have mistaken correlation for causation.

All presently accepted psychological theories are based on certain assumptions of cause and effect. These theories are tested on the basis of hypotheses that have been developed from the same underlying assumptions. The most interesting and productive thing for us as behavioral scientists to do is to look more closely at where these assumptions originated. If we were to do this, we would discover that assumptions are conditioned forms of thought. Lack of this understanding has impeded our progress as psychologists. Instead of developing an understanding of thought systems and how these systems shape our experience, we attempt to analyze the content of our own conditioned experience by using the content of our own conditioned thinking!

THOUGHT AND CONDITIONING: CAUSE AND EFFECT

As human beings, we are capable of attaching or associating any event (experience) with any other event in terms of cause and effect because of the nature of our biological computer. The human brain is a biological computer that can be programmed with any information. It does not matter to the brain whether the information is true or false; the brain merely accepts and stores information in memory. The brain, in and of itself, has no ability to discern the factualness of information. This ability is a function of the individual's level of consciousness. Once data have been programmed into memory, the brain, depending on the individual's level of consciousness at any given moment, will respond in accord with that information. In other words, the content of human thought can be conditioned.

Ivan Pavlov, the famous Russian scientist, found that he could program a dog to connect the sound of a bell with the appearance of food, so that the animal would salivate at the sound of the bell, even in the absence of food. In essence, Pavlov had accidentally discovered how the condition of illusion, or misinformation, could be programmed into experience. Unknowingly, he discovered how conditioning creates separate realities. But instead of realizing the implications that this discovery has pertaining to a human being's *capability* to be programmed with information, and what that means in terms of human experience, the field, already caught up in a conditioned reality has directed its efforts toward explaining every aspect of the *effect* of conditioning. The field has lost sight of the larger picture and put its efforts into developing a behavioral technology with which to condition people's experiences and has failed to recognize and address the basic fact of conditioning itself. Part of the result of the field of psychology overlooking the fact that human thought can be conditioned is that we have patients who have accepted the belief that sanity and insanity are habits. Thus millions of patients undergo treatment aimed at reprogramming them but are never directed to look at the implications of the fact that they are capable of being programmed in the first place.

Rather than pointing to the relative and illusory quality of all conditioned behavior, which would have the effect of freeing people from seeing their beliefs and reactions as fixed and absolute, the field has created theories to explain the results of conditioning within a framework that has not allowed the field to see beyond the limits of its own thoughts on the subject. In essence, once the field of psychology became fascinated with the byproducts of conditioning, then theories, models, and techniques had to be constructed to treat these byproducts. So, because individuals are capable of associating any event to any other event, in terms of cause and effect, they are also capable of creating an infinite number of suppositions about the causes of behavior. Once a supposition has been made and accepted by others in the field, these suppositions, true or false, eventually become the basis of theories, models, or treatment modalities. Once a supposition achieves the status of a psychological theory and is promoted as a fact by the psychological "experts," society accepts them into its belief system and these theories become part of our expectations, perceptions, and reactions. People in the society, to varying degrees, accept these views and begin to behave in ways that are consistent with the perceptions that those ideas foster. In other words, behavioral scientists use their ability to think to create an idea that eventually becomes a theory, which in turn has a high potential for becoming a reality for many people.

Quite often, behavioral scientists will theorize about a certain cause-and-effect relationship and then proceed to carry out research to validate their theory. The problem is that in the absence of recognizing that thought shapes reality, social scientists engaged in such research have not taken into consideration possible contamination such as demand characteristics or experimenter bias.

Demand characteristics refer to the beliefs, expectations, and perceptions that subjects in psychological experiments bring with them to the experiment that promote compliance with the experimenter's wishes. In one study,[1] for example, psychologist Stanley Milgram was amazed to find that volunteers in one of his psychological experiments were willing to administer what they believed to be dangerous and severely painful high-voltage shocks to other subjects, despite the subjects' desperate pleas and demands to be excused from the experiment. Another similar study[2] involved some subjects who were "hypnotized" and some who were not. There were four groups in this study: Group 1 subjects were hypnotized; Group 2 subjects (simulators) were not hypnotized but were told that they were serving as a control group and that their role was to fool the experimenter by pretending to be in a deep trance; Group 3 subjects (nonsimulators) were also told they were a control group but were not asked to simulate being hypnotized; Group 4 subjects were not told that they were in an experiment and nothing was said about hypnosis.

All subjects in this experiment were then asked to perform a

variety of incredibly dangerous and foolish tasks. One task involved the subjects being shown a rattlesnake in a cage. The subject was then asked to reach in and touch it. After being shown a
beaker of nitric acid and watching a coin dissolve in it, the subjects
were asked to reach in and retrieve the coin. Finally, they were
asked to throw the acid in the experimenter's face. The experiment, of course, was set up so that no one could be hurt, but the
subjects did not know this. As expected, Group 1 subjects (hypnotized) produced high compliance, with 84% performing all
three tasks. Surprisingly, Group 3 subjects (nonsimulators) also
exhibited high compliance, with 50% performing the task of
touching the rattle snake and 84% performing the two tasks involving the nitric acid. Totally amazing, however, was the fact that
100% of the subjects in Group 2, (simulators), who were told to
fake being in a trance, performed all the tasks. The power of
wanting to be a compliant subject was highlighted by the fact that
none of the subjects in Group 4—those who did not know that
they were in an experiment—would perform any of what appeared
to them to be dangerous and nonsensical tasks.

The common belief is that subjects in psychological experiments are "naive" or neutral participants if they have never partic-
ipated in an experiment and perhaps have never even taken a
psychology course before. But are they? Obviously not. Participants in experiments bring with them beliefs that psychologists or
scientists are authorities whom one should listen to, trust, and
obey. *

Experimenter bias, on the other hand, refers to the influence

---

* The new level of understanding of the studies being presented in this book is
providing mental health professionals with a fresh perspective on the extreme
compliance exhibited by people who join cults or appear to be "brainwashed"
(for example, the Jonestown incident in which over 900 people committed suicide). Such high levels of compliance seem to be more a result of people's level
of insecurity and lack of understanding of thought, than the techniques used by
cult leaders.

which the experimenter has on experimental results, even under controlled conditions. In a series of studies,[3] psychologist Robert Rosenthal showed the almost universal effect of the experimenter's beliefs. In school settings, students whom the teacher thinks are brighter do better than others, even though the students do not actually differ in intelligence. This effect has been demonstrated in even simple learning experiments with rats. If an experimenter is told that certain rats are smarter than others, the "smart" rats do better than other rats even though there is no actual difference.

Both demand characteristics and experimenter bias show how thought, at a low level of understanding of how it functions, shapes reality. The first case refers to the subject's reality, the second to the experimenter's reality. When one looks at the above studies, it is difficult not to recognize that the same pattern is occurring between clinician and patient (remember "On Being Sane in Insane Places" in Chapter 1?), professor and student, parent and child.

Take the case of George, presented in the first chapter. In all likelihood, George, in search of his mental health, would have willingly, but unknowingly stepped into any one of the separate realities being offered by the four therapists. What we are trying to do is direct the field of mental health to look at the fact that people in society are looking for their sanity using, as their guide, the thoughts that the experts in our field provide and promote. There are hundreds of millions of people who are doing this. This is why it is a blessing when an "expert" wakes up to a deeper understanding.

THE CONDITIONED NATURE OF CONCEPTS AND THEORIES

Throughout the history of psychology, we have focussed on specific factors or variables that we have come to think are important.

165

Consequently, we have constructed theories that relate behaviors, perceptions, and problems to these arbitrary variables. We then focus on these variables in our research, our teaching, and our counseling. What we find, however, is that this focus does not produce the results we seek.

What we have begun to realize is that all theories and models are concepts that have come from the thought system of the founder of that theory. An example of this phenomenon is the consensus for the field of psychology of the work of Sigmund Freud. In order to explain human behavior, Freud created, among other things, the idea of the id, ego, and superego. He described what these entities were and how they operated. He then created a method of treatment based on these concepts. People have assumed that Freud discovered and described some fixed, absolute reality. These people fail to realize that he did not *discover* the id, the ego, or the superego, but that he *created* these constructs from his personal thought. In other words, he developed these concepts to explain his personal ideas about human behavior. In time, this thinking was accepted, not only by the field at large, but also by millions of people who complied by thinking of and perceiving life in Freudian terms.

Since all psychological theories are in themselves systems of thought, the answer to a more advanced psychology cannot be found within the content boundaries of any particular theory. The proliferation of theories in present-day psychology is in itself a sign of the frustration of the field trying to break through to an answer within the context of the framework of its basic assumptions. Yet behind all these theories is the function of thought that was used to create the assumptions of the various theories.

One of the characteristics of a thought system is that the content of that system will remain internally consistent and the thinker, by virtue of seeing reality in terms of his or her own beliefs, will function to maintain the validity of that content. This is especially true when the individual is oblivious to that fact that he or she is thinking. A thought system is not capable of presenting arguments against its own content. The thinking of any system of thought will not tell us to question the validity of the content of that system. On the contrary, all thinking that results from that system will maintain the integrity of the content of that system.

THE MYTH OF INFORMATION

In the absence of recognizing that thinking is the formulator of people's experience, the mental health professional has gathered more and more information regarding people's problems. This is why the study of human behavior comes up with more causes, more types of traumas, more neuroses, more syndromes, and more categories and classifications of disturbances. Even though we continue to identify, catalogue, and document symptomatic details and varieties of emotional problems, the answers that we seek elude us. This is because the solution that we seek does not lie in categorized details of conditioned thought. Rather, the solution lies in realizing a more profound understanding of the nature of thought and the power thought has to create personal experience in life.

This is why information alone cannot produce the answers that we seek. If the answers we seek could be found in information, we should have them by now because there is no shortage of information. There are already thousands of libraries, microfilm files, and computers storing countless descriptive studies on human behavior in every kind of situation, condition, and group. There are refinements of studies that are themselves refinements of other studies. Information abounds on television, in newspapers, in computers, in dissertations and journals.

More information about what we do not understand is of very limited value. Rather, solutions will be realized when we are willing to take a more objective look at how we create information in the first place.

THE RELATIVE NATURE OF PSYCHOLOGICAL INQUIRY

Similarly, scientific methodology alone will not lead us to the answer. Scientific methodology can only ensure relative objectivity. That is, it can only guarantee consistency and reliability in how we gather data. What the scientific method cannot guarantee is that our data will be valid or that we will understand the data that we gather. The only guarantee is that whatever data we collect will be valid within the relative limits of the understanding that defines and interprets the measurements that are made.

The predicament of early astronomers illustrates this point. In the early days of astronomy, the science had an underlying assumption that the earth was the fixed and stationary center of the universe. Thus all studies and observations were carried out within this frame of reference. So, when astronomers were first charting the movement of the planets and the stars, these scientists did so under the assumption that the earth was a stationary center from which these measurements were being made. Astronomers objectively described their observations, innocent of the fact that they, too, were moving because of the orbit and rotation of the earth. In other words, they did not take into account the fact that they were an indisputable part of the field that they were observing. Thus, even though their measurements were accurate, the model of the physical universe that these astronomers derived from their studies was valid only if one assumed that the earth was stationary. When all of the data were pooled, the resulting formulations were relatively true, yet they were far from factual. The equations and formulas derived from observing the movements of heavenly bodies were based on a faulty basic premise. Then, from this faulty premise, studies were designed to discover more about what was believed to be true. Scientists hoped to discover more about this pattern. Research and the resulting equations became more and more complicated and disparate, with larger margins of error. Different theories and models were created to account for the variance. Ironically, all of the problems and inconsistencies within the field of astronomy at that time were, in fact, self-generated. The solution to the problem was realized only when the field began to question its assumptions and see the relativity of its measurements.

When Nicholas Copernicus derived the notion that the earth was not the center of the universe, but rather that the planets revolved around the sun, there was a compelling logic in this notion for those scientists who were truly looking for an answer rather than protecting a theory, because it simplified and conformed to the patterns of what had been observed. The change in the frame of reference of astronomy suddenly made all of the equations simple and consistent in describing the movements of the planets relative to the earth, the stars, and the sun.

The field of psychology is in the same predicament as the early astronomers. Although sincerely attempting to find solutions for psychological problems, the field has been unable to provide simple, consistent answers for human psychological difficulties. Rigorous research methodology continues to be utilized in the behavioral sciences, and yet no significant breakthrough has been realized. A breakthrough has not occurred because the answers to the riddles have nothing to do with the objectivity of our research methodology, but rather with the underlying assumptions of our questions. *We are measuring ourselves with our own theories, models, and assumptions.* We have failed to realize that these are already biased measurements. As far as objectivity goes, we are too late the moment we study our behaviors using an arbitrary and relative set of beliefs as the basis for measurement. Confined to, and believing completely in, the currently accepted frame of reference of psychological thinking, we have not taken into account the role that thinking played in formulating our version of reality. In short, we have lost sight of the fact that we are part of the field that we are studying.

The answers that the field is seeking will be realized when we understand that all theories, concepts, assumptions, and information are byproducts of a personal thought system. Each psychological formulation comes directly from the conditioned separate reality of the formulator of that theory. When we begin to see this larger picture, we will be led back to the basic principles of human functioning. At that point the field will take a step out of confusion and diversity and move toward simplicity.

MOVING TOWARD SIMPLICITY

The way out of the confusion is simple. It is difficult to grasp only because our present thinking will not point outside of itself. But as we learn about the psychological function of thought and how we use this function to create perceptions, assumptions, theories, concepts, information, and beliefs, we will begin to cut through the confusion inherent in these byproducts of psychological functioning to see, in simplicity, the functioning itself. This understanding leads us outside our personal, conditioned frame of reference to one which is larger, one which encompasses all the rest.

The Need for an Advanced Psychology

Einstein shocked the field of physics by proving that there was no absolute inertial or physical frame of reference. In other words, everything is in motion relative to everything else. Similarly, since the personal reality is derived from an individualized thought system there is no absolute psychological frame of reference to be found within the context of the separate reality of any individual. What does exist, however, are objective, impersonal facts or principles of how separate realities are formed and maintained to create reality. These principles show us the nature and function of personal thought. Psychological principles reveal the basic capability possessed by every human being, the *ability* to think. This ability includes the power to create an infinite variety of thought content and then to believe or disbelieve our creation. These principles show us the power of believed thought to create reality or personal experience in life. They reveal how people move in and out of certain states of mind where they cannot see beyond the reality of their own thinking. They show us the role of feelings in maintaining healthy functional states. These basic principles of human functioning apply consistently across all separate conceptual frameworks to define the nature and function of these intellectual frameworks.

Albert Einstein saw things in simplicity. His original principles were simple, but profound. As people began to grasp the meaning of the principles that he presented, people saw how these principles were connected to every form of physical phenomenon. Similarly, once we begin to grasp the simple principles of human psychological functioning, we begin to see how these principles are connected to all forms of human reasoning and experience. When we begin to understand the principles of psychological relativity, we will once again be brought back to the fact of our own thinking. We will realize that as we are measuring any reality (individual or field), we are simultaneously creating that reality through our thinking function. Understanding this fact will break the field through to a new dimension of inquiry.

The field of psychology is on the verge of this discovery. More and more the field is exploring areas such as consciousness, mind, psychosomatic medicine, and cognition. Yet we as a field have merely scratched the surface in terms of our understanding of the power of human thought. In order to evolve to something beyond what we already think, we must look beyond the information, theories, assumptions, and methods that are the form this thinking has taken. This process involves setting aside the current psychological frame of reference in order to see something beyond it. Thinking that we already know the answer because we possess so much information is the greatest barrier to learning something new. Psychology will have to be willing to step outside the boundaries of its own theoretical field to see how this field came into existence in the first place. At this point, psychology will break through to become the most potent source of mental help that this culture has ever known.

CHAPTER ELEVEN

Today's Psychology: A Level of Consciousness

It was inevitable that our desire to understand ourselves psychologically, from intellectual systems of thought, would result in the production of an immense quantity of diverse ideas and approaches. It was also inevitable that as a field, we would organize these ideas into a formal discipline of study, which in turn, would become a reference source for understanding human behavior. What has happened is that we now look at this collection of quite arbitrary ideas about human behavior and the tools with which to measure behavior as if they were a set of facts about our mental and emotional functioning as human beings.

However, all of our theories, approaches, and tools are products of our level of understanding in relation to our ability to think. These thoughts, as is the nature of thought at a given level of consciousness have become self-validating. They shape the reality of the therapist, the profession, and the science. If, for example, therapists believe that people's problems come from traumatic events in their early childhood, they will unearth events that they see as traumatic and then show a consistent cause-and-effect relationship between those events and present behaviors. This is possible because human beings can use thought to connect unrelated events and then perceive that their connection is factual.

Most therapists have innocently accepted theories, including techniques and tools, from their teachers without questioning how these theories came into existence in the first place. These theories then get passed from the therapist to the client, who, once again, accepts them without question or regard to how they originated. Thus present-day psychological training consists of professionals teaching their students to accept their beliefs and perceptions of why people are what they are. Without knowing any better, students, who are predisposed to compliance to begin with, end up identifying with the theoretical views they have learned and become the new generation of teachers. This is how a level of consciousness is perpetuated.

Thought systems are not limited to individual people, but also exist and operate in an identical manner in any group or organization of people, such as a profession or a science. The big problem now is that we, as mental health professionals consider the products of the profession—the theories, the tests, and the therapeutic techniques—as being essential to, if not synonomous with, the science. They are not. Anything that we, as mental health professionals, have produced to date represents the best, given our level of understanding at the time. It stands to reason that, as our understanding increases, the nature of our theories, our products, and our therapies will also change.

SCIENTIFIC BREAKTHROUGHS: A NEW LEVEL OF CONSCIOUSNESS

Advancement in the field of psychology requires that we as a field break through the barriers of our own thought system. It is understandable and predictable that every field of study will begin to stagnate or limit itself within its own conceptual framework. The signs of this happening are a further refinement of what is known into categories and subcategories with finer degrees of specialization and differentiation between specialties. A breakdown in objectivity is evidenced by the formation of different, even conflicting, schools of thought, each defining its own interpretation of the data.

Throughout history, breakthroughs have occurred in every culture, society, institution, science, family, and individual. A discovery or breakthrough occurs when the status quo is seen for what it is and a higher level is recognized. There are countless examples of breakthroughs in history—the discoveries of Columbus, Galileo, Pasteur, Lister, Bell, Einstein, Edison, and Ford are just a few. The recognition of a breakthrough in a field raises the level of understanding, which in turn serves to integrate and to clarify the relationship of the existing data, regardless of how fragmented the data may appear to be. A breakthrough will unify and define the fragments into laws or principles.

Interestingly, all scientific breakthroughs have been resisted by the very scientists who were supposedly searching for new knowledge. To most people, the persecution of great discoverers such as Galileo by their peers is not a new topic. What is surprising for many, however, is finding out that such persecution was not restricted to medieval times. Few realize, for example, the degree of personal attack that Albert Einstein withstood as a result of introducing the theory of relativity. The most recent example is that of Immanuel Velikovsky, who invoked the wrath of the field of astronomy by proposing in the 1950s a new and controversial theory concerning the earth and the development of the solar system. Psychologist Michael Mahoney described Velikovsky's experience this way:

Velikovsky described the derivation of his theory as well as specifying several potential tests of its accuracy. Despite his repeated attempts to stimulate research, Velikovsky was snubbed by hundreds of scientists—some of whom refused to even read his theory. The popular press picked up some of the sensational aspects of the theory, and diatribes against Velikovsky were soon offered by scores of his colleagues. He was not allowed to publish rebuttals, even when some of his astronomical claims had been unexpectedly verified by his detractors. After rejections from many other publishers, the Macmillan Company agreed to publish a book version of Velikovsky's ideas, titled *Worlds in Collision*.[1] When word got out that a contract had been offered, the Macmillan Company began to receive threats from the scientific community. After some hesitation, Macmillan went ahead with publication—and immediately felt the wrath of organized science. Their other books were boycotted and their sales representatives were refused appointments at several major universities. Letters demanding cessation of publication were received. In response to this book, the American Association for the Advancement of Science proposed that future publications of new scientific hypotheses be restricted to authors who could claim sponsorship from "a proper professional body." Individuals who voiced tolerance or support for Velikovsky's views—such as the Chairman of the Astronomy Department at the American Museum of Natural History—were threatened with being fired if they did not withdraw their support. The pressure finally became so great that the Macmillan Company capitulated. They ceased publication and sold their rights to the manuscript. Several years later, Velikovsky documented the verification of several of his "preposterous" claims. . . . The issue, of course, is not whether Velikovsky was correct. The fact that he was so energetically persecuted and denied access to means for rebutting his critics is a sad chapter in the history of science.[2]

Why do scientists so often resist new discoveries when, in fact, such discoveries represent progress? The basic reason for such resistance is that new discoveries are not always seen for what they are because they bring with them a new reality. If you will remember, in Chapter 6 we noted that the ego state is not limited to individuals, but also exists for groups of people. This is why new discoveries often threaten people's egos—their image of who they think they are. Scientists and the sciences they comprise often fall victim to the ego state of mind. Thus, for scientists whose self-esteem, reputation, authority, security, and identity are attached to a theory, a breakthrough to a new reality is indeed a threatening and often maddening event. Luckily, the history of science illustrates that while new discoveries always meet with resistance from the "old guard," these discoveries are irresistible to the younger scientist and the open-minded.

In order for the field of psychology to break through its limited field of thought, it must be willing to take a fresh look at its most basic assumptions about human behavior. At the very least, the field must be willing to question the validity of its present beliefs, assumptions, approaches, and products.

THE CIRCLE OF SEARCH AND RESEARCH

What today's psychological research accomplishes is to describe the commonly held meanings which people predictably, at the prevailing levels of understanding, give to different events. What the researcher and theorist have not fully realized is that it is only these meanings that we ourselves unknowingly give to our past or to our present experience that determine the degree of mental health that we enjoy at the moment. So, it is the present level of understanding of the field of psychology that prevents it from recognizing how humanity's separate realities are created.

The most basic problem with this level of reasoning is that, once again, every thought system is an internally consistent and, to varying degrees, self-validating reality. What this means is that each of us operates on the basis of a specific framework of beliefs. Furthermore, we do so at a given level of conscious understanding about the reality of those beliefs. Accordingly, we then experience situations in a manner consistent with this reality. That is, we make certain interpretations of situations and arrive at certain conclusions that conform to our belief system. If we remain at a level of consciousness where we ignore the fact that we are making up interpretations as we go along, then we will be compelled by an unchanging belief system to experience the same scientific patterns, with different details, continually throughout our lives.

As a result of our present psychological misconceptions, we have yet to realize the circularity of our theoretical reasonings. Objectivity has been interpreted as consistency and reliability in the interpretation of research data. As a result of this, the use of what is known as "scientific method" in psychological research has been unable to bring objectivity to the field, for the simple fact that the data of psychology are theoretical. That is, we assign a quantitative value to some event or process outside the control of the individual and say that that factor is what causes certain behaviors. Thus the fact that we consistently and reliably assign quantitative values to something which is based on theory has been interpreted as a sign of objectivity. However, nothing could be further from the truth.

Presently, researchers design and carry out their research in line with their theories. In most cases, as was noted in Chapter 10, each researcher finds support for his or her particular view. This is one of the reasons why theories are never discarded from the ever accumulating collection. These theories and their conclusions are then used as the conceptual bases for further research, and thus become incorporated into the frame of reference of how human beings are understood.

BEYOND THE LEVEL OF PSYCHOLOGY TODAY

Results from research that merely tests the consistency and reliability of what we already know is of no value in offering something new or efficacious to the field of mental health. Treatment programs that are based on these results will only serve to reinforce and to maintain the overall belief system of the field. All theories now accepted in the field are based on certain assumptions of cause and effect and are tested on the basis of hypotheses developed from the same assumptions. The assumptions are that people's problems come from their pasts, their psychological makeup, or their circumstances. Given this frame of reference, the field of psychology surfaces more examples of problems and then verifies their causes within the existing theoretical framework.

These assumptions overlook what occurs, moment to moment, as people move from one frame of reference to another. Adherence to these basic assumptions acts as a barrier to understanding how thought is related to experience in life, or how it is possible to change our minds (our thought systems) in our evolution to higher states of consciousness.

As we will further illustrate in the next chapter, the same level of thought is built into every facet of psychology—the theories, the therapies, the research, and the testing. This is why a breakthrough is needed in the field as a whole, so that all these areas of psychology will be given a new level of validity. This is why we have discussed the present circularity of thinking in psychology, so that through this more encompassing recognition, a new level of understanding can be achieved.

THEORY AND PSYCHOLOGICAL TESTING

Psychological tests are interesting phenomena because they are one of the links in the circularity of traditional thinking. To begin with, psychological tests were derived from theories of psychological functioning. These tests were then used in the process of validating the theories from which they originated. New tests that are developed must be "cross-validated" with "established" tests in order to be considered valid. Clinically, these tests are then adopted as a means through which clinicians can validate their understanding of their clients.

Most psychological tests used today fall under the categories of what are referred to as "projective" or "objective" tests. These designations, however, are misleading. Contrary to what most people believe, the terms *projective* or *objective* refer to the format of the test itself and not to any objective quality of the test logic or results. For example, if a test requires that the person taking it interpret pictures or inkblot designs, the test is considered to be projective. That is, the person's interpretations are considered by the examiner as a projection of an internal psychic state. On the other hand, if the test format consists of questions for which there are "norms" and whose scoring is standardized, the test is considered to be objective in nature.

What many people do not realize is that the test results of both projective and objective tests are based on *interpretations* and an interpretation has nothing necessarily to do with the condition of the person that is taking the test. Rather, such interpretation comes from the separate reality of either the author of the test or the person making the interpretation of what the client's responses mean. The interpretation, in other words, depends on the theoretical orientation of the psychometrist.

The reason why this is not common knowledge is that the consumer of psychological tests, typically a nonpsychologist, is rarely in a position to openly question or become informed about psychological tests. The nonpsychologist typically sees only the test form and an interpretation. However, there are instances in which the lay public does have a chance to look behind the curtain and glimpse the logic behind the interpretations that psychologists give test results. One such instance was highlighted by sociologist Ray Jeffrey,[3] who wrote a sobering article addressing the pitfalls in assuming that psychological tests are totally valid. Jeffrey submitted two examples of how psychological tests stand up to a series of logical questions. The following are excerpts from the two criminal cases used in Jeffrey's article, in which psychologists utilized psychological tests as the foundation for establishing that the defendants in these cases were insane and unable to control behavior.

Case No. 1[4]

Prosecuting Attorney: What did the House-Tree-Person Test reveal? [This is a projective test in which the subject is asked to draw a house, a tree, and a person. The psychologist then interprets the subject's response in terms of sanity or insanity.]

Psychologist A: The major finding was a feeling of withdrawal, running away from reality, feelings of rejection by women.

Prosecuting Attorney: And the results of the Szondi? [This is a test in which the subject selects pictures of people he or she likes and dislikes. The people pictured are mentally disturbed.]

Psychologist A: This showed a passive, depressed person who withdrew from the world of reality, with an inability to relate to the world of others.

Prosecuting Attorney: Wasn't the Szondi Test made up around 1900? or the early 1900 period? And wasn't it made up of [pictures of] a number of Europeans who were acutely psychotic?

Psychologist A: Yes, that is true.

Prosecuting Attorney: And this tells you something about his personality?

Psychologist A: Yes, you can tell something about the person from his responses to the photos.

Prosecuting Attorney: And the House-Tree-Person Test—you handed the defendant Kent a pencil and a blank piece of paper, is that right, Doctor?

Psychologist A: That is correct.

Prosecuting Attorney: And you asked him to draw a house?

Psychologist A: Yes.

Prosecuting Attorney: And what did this tell you about Kent?

Psychologist A: The absence of a door, and the bars on the windows, indicated he saw the house as a jail, not a home. Also, you will notice it is a side view of the house; he was making it inaccessible.

Prosecuting Attorney: Isn't it normal to draw a side view of a house? You didn't ask him to draw a front view, did you?

Psychologist A: No.

Prosecuting Attorney: And those bars on the window—could they have been Venetian blinds and not bars? Who called them bars, you or Kent?

Psychologist A: I did.

Prosecuting Attorney: Did you ask him what they were?

Psychologist A: No.

Prosecuting Attorney: What else did the drawing reveal about Kent?

Psychologist A: The line in front of the house runs from left to right. This indicates a need for security.

Prosecuting Attorney: This line indicates insecurity! Could it also indicate the contour of the landscape, like a lawn or something?

Psychologist A: This is not the interpretation I gave it.

Prosecuting Attorney: And the chimney—what does it indicate?

Psychologist A: You will notice the chimney is dark. This indicates disturbed sexual feelings. The smoke indicates inner daydreaming.

Prosecuting Attorney: Did I understand you correctly? Did you say dark chimneys indicate disturbed sex feelings?

Psychologist A: Yes.

Prosecuting Attorney: Then you asked him to draw a person?

Psychologist A: Yes.

Prosecuting Attorney: And he drew this picture of a male?

Psychologist A: Yes.

Prosecuting Attorney: And what does this drawing indicate about Kent?

Psychologist A: The man appears to be running. This indicates anxiety, agitation. He is running, you will notice, to the left. This indicates running away from the environment. If he had been running to the right this would indicate entering the environment. [The reader should note that this same psychologist previously stated that a line drawn from left to right signified a need for security.]

Prosecuting Attorney: How about the hands?

Psychologist A: The sharp fingers may indicate hostility.

Prosecuting Attorney: Anything else?

Psychologist A: The head and body appear to be separated by a dark collar, and the neck is long. This indicates a split between intellect and emotion. The dark hair, dark tie, dark shoes, and dark buckle indicate anxiety about sexual problems.

Prosecuting Attorney: You then asked Kent to draw a person of the opposite sex. What did this picture indicate?

Psychologist A: The dark piercing eyes indicated a feeling of rejection by women, hostility toward women.

Prosecuting Attorney: Did you administer the Szondi Test, Doctor?

Psychologist B: No. I don't happen to think much of it. The test assumes a schizophrenic looks a certain way, and we have evidence that this isn't so. [The reader will note that this stands in direct contradiction to the view of Psychologist A, who felt this test was valid enough to substantiate his testimony.]

Prosecuting Attorney: What responses did you receive from Kent on the Rorschach, the inkblot test? [This is the classic "inkblot" test. Different inkblot patterns are shown to the subject, who is asked to tell the examiner what each reminds him of.]

Psychologist B: Wolf, butterfly, vagina, pelvis, bats, buttocks, etc.

Prosecuting Attorney: And from this you concluded the defendant was schizophrenic?

Psychologist B: Yes, [from] that and other things.

Prosecuting Attorney: You gave him the Wechsler Adult Scale? [This is the most widely used IQ test for adults.]

Psychologist B: Yes.

Prosecuting Attorney: Now you asked the defendant to define blood vessels, did you not?

Psychologist B: Yes.

Prosecuting Attorney: And his answer was capillaries and veins. You scored him zero. Why? Aren't capillaries and veins blood vessels?

Psychologist B: I don't know. The norms don't consider that answer acceptable.

Prosecuting Attorney: What norms?

Psychologist B: You see, these tests are scored on the basis of norms secured by administering the test to thousands of people.

Prosecuting Attorney: On the comprehension section you asked Kent: "If you found a sealed, addressed, stamped envelope on the street, what would you do with it?" and he answered "Turn it in." Why did you give him a 1? Why not a 2?

Psychologist B: Because of the norms. A 2-answer would require more—something like "Mail it" or "Take it to the post office."

Prosecuting Attorney: You asked him "What does the phrase 'Strike while the iron is hot' mean?" What was his answer?

Psychologist B: "Strike when it is best to strike." I gave him a zero.

Prosecuting Attorney: Why? Doesn't "Strike when the iron is hot" mean to strike when the opportunity presents itself?

Psychologist B: In terms of the norms it is not an acceptable answer.

Prosecuting Attorney: You asked Kent: "What is similar about the eye and ear?" and he said "They are organs." You gave him a 1. Why?

Psychologist B: Because a 2-answer is more precise, such as "organs of perception."

Prosecuting Attorney: You asked the defendant to draw a human figure?

Psychologist C: Yes.

Prosecuting Attorney: And this is the figure he drew for you? What does it indicate about his personality?

Psychologist C: You will note this is a rear view of a male. This is very rare, statistically. It indicates hiding guilt feeling, or turning away from reality.

Prosecuting Attorney: And this drawing of a female figure, does it indicate anything to you, and if so, what?

Psychologist C: It indicates hostility towards women on the part of the subject. The pose, the hands on the hips, the hard-looking face, the stern expression.

Prosecuting Attorney: Anything else?

Psychologist C: The size of the ears indicates a paranoid outlook or hallucinations. Also, the absence of feet indicates feelings of insecurity.

Prosecuting Attorney: On the Wechsler, you asked him: "What

187

would you do if you found a sealed, addressed, stamped envelope?" And he answered: "Open it and find out who it belongs to. I will show you I know right from wrong." [This is the same subject who answered "Turn it in" to the previous psychologist.]

Prosecuting Attorney: Do you usually arrive at the diagnosis on the basis of one Rorschach administered twice within an hour?

Psychologist D: Frequently.

Prosecuting Attorney: What else in the drawing is significant psychologically?

Psychologist D: The irregularity or sketchiness of the lines may suggest tension and anxiety. The attention paid to details—to the belt-bow-tie, and pockets—indicate a little-boy-like quality about the defendant.

Prosecuting Attorney: Is it significant that the figure is running to the left, and not to the right?

Psychologist D: To some people, yes. I don't place any significance on it.

Prosecuting Attorney: On the basis of these responses, you concluded the defendant was schizophrenic?

Psychologist D: Yes.

Case No. 2[5]

Prosecuting Attorney: Doctor, do you agree with this statement: "It is well established that psychiatrists and psychologists freely concede there is no absolute accuracy and reliability of tests in the measurement of intelligence."

Psychologist A: I do not agree.

Prosecuting Attorney: How about this statement: "Two persons of substantially the same mental capacity may test with materially different scores or rating depending on education, training, and environment, etc."

Psychologist A: Well, environment includes so much that I would think this would affect the performance on intelligence tests.

Prosecuting Attorney: You can tell from responses to Rorschach cards what his [the defendant's] personality is like?

Psychologist A: From a global picture.

Prosecuting Attorney: What response did he give to Card 4?

Psychologist A: He saw a frog.

Prosecuting Attorney: And what significance did you attach to this answer, Doctor?

Psychologist A: This is not the response normal people give. People often see two boots.

Prosecuting Attorney: Why do you use pictures of insane people on the Szondi? Why not normal subjects?

Psychologist A: We know penicillin works; we don't know why it works. It's the same thing here. We know that certain kinds of tests work; we don't understand why they work. [The reader will note that the means by which penicillin as well as the other anti-biotics inhibit or destroy bacteria are in fact well known.]

Prosecuting Attorney: What do you mean by adequate controls?

Psychologist B: When the tensions build up in him [the subject] to a state of anxiety, anger, frustration, his emotions explode into behavior over which he has no control.

Prosecuting Attorney: Do you believe in free will?

Psychologist B: That is a philosophic, not a psychological, problem. Free will is an arbitrary, sudden explosion without cause. I don't believe that. If I am free to choose, why is it I choose one thing and you choose another? It is because of the structure of the nervous system, and the influence of the environment. . . .

Court Judge: Any individual is free to make a choice, isn't he?

Psychologist B: Yes.

Prosecuting Attorney: Why did you use photographs of mentally ill persons—why not normal persons?

Psychologist B: Because photographs of mentally ill persons are supposed to accentuate the needs or drives or deprivations or frustrations that human beings experience. Normal people have managed to resolve their frustrations. I don't know why it works. It is something underneath. It is difficult to explain and understand. Doctors use digitalis for heart disease without knowing why it acts as it does. [The reader will note that the action of digitalis on the heart function is well known.]

[After further questioning concerning the Szondi test, the judge threw the test cards down. The defense then requested that the record reflect this action.]

Court Judge: The record may reflect it, but the record may show I am throwing it [the psychological testimony based on the Szondi] all out. That will take care of that session.

The fact that all psychological tests involve arbitrary, subjective, theoretical interpretations is not always apparent, since some tests have been standardized with regard to the interpretations given to a particular test pattern or response. This, however, does not change the subjective nature of the instrument. Standardizing a psychological test (i.e., establishing "norms") means that most of the professionals following a particular theory agree on a certain interpretation. We forget, however, that prior to Columbus, the vast majority of the Western world agreed that the world was flat. Indeed, this belief was standardized in the culture and was consistent with the theories and data of the times.

In essence, what most psychological tests do is translate human conditions such as retardation, criminality, anxiety, depression, or anger, into the complex psychological terms of a particular theory. As a result of these theoretical explanations, many people become consumers of therapies or programs for conditions which are assumed to be the remedy for a problem that the tests supposedly uncovered. Every therapist has seen clients who have developed clinical self-images. These clients can give complicated explanations why they exhibit certain behaviors and feelings. Unfortunately, this only serves to keep clients living within those versions of reality.

Naturally, the development or use of inventories is not wrong or ill advised. What we are pointing out is that the majority of present-day psychological inventories were derived from antiquated theories of human behavior that anchored people to their problems, their past, their personalities, and, in essence, their limitations. Consequently, evaluation tools derived from these theories tend to lock people into the very realities that those individuals wish to change. When the field recognizes this, a more factual level of psychological understanding will be realized, and more factual and practical tests will be developed.

INTELLIGENCE TESTS

Intelligence tests provide a good example of why our tools are in need of revision and replacement. An intelligence test measures a person's ability to recall memorized information pertaining to cultural literature, history, geography, vocabulary, and arithmetic. This ability is considered to be "verbal intelligence." Likewise, these tests measure a person's ability to duplicate and/or complete different varieties of puzzles. This ability is considered to be "performance intelligence." Designating such measures as representing people's intelligence quotients (IQs) is a misuse of the term "intelligence" and has produced some interesting questions. Why, for example, do people who have equivalent IQ scores act unequally intelligent? Why does a person with a high score often lack common sense or wisdom? Why is it that intelligence, as measured in these tests, does not ensure happiness or success in life? Why is it that "high intelligence," as defined by psychological tests, does not mean that a person will not produce feelings of anxiety, depression, insecurity, stress, delusions, prejudice, anger, hate, hostility, jealousy, or envy? Why is it that a superior intelligence will not ensure that an individual will not fight, steal, kill, or commit suicide? Why haven't high IQ's of the leaders in this world solved international problems?

These are interesting questions. In fact, what psychology today calls "intelligence" doesn't even pretend to correlate with mental health. The only thing that a high score on an intelligence test will predict is how well that person will do on tasks that are similar to the items on the test. In fact, a high IQ score will predict that the individual with that score will score high on other intelligence tests.

We are not saying that testing is wrong. The important point is to understand the limitations of testing. What IQ tests are in fact measuring is the information-processing capability of the brain under certain circumstances. A useful function of such tests is in the area of neurological testing.

As a scientific field, we must at some point take a look at what we are doing in this area. We need to recognize that there is a more profound and true intelligence than what we have previously recognized—an intelligence that can guide us to use more creatively and positively the information that we have at our disposal for the benefit of ourselves and our society. Information, regardless of how voluminous or sophisticated, in the absence of the deeper intelligence that we are calling common sense or wisdom, is of absolutely no value in guiding us in our evolution. Information without common sense can be used to create and spread antagonism, superstition, prejudice, and the negative rigidities that guard such ignorance. We must begin to recognize that there is a deeper intelligence that is correlated, not with information stored in the biological computer, but with the state of mental health. With this recognition, the field of psychology will have something of value to offer society.

STRESS TESTS

Recent newcomers to the arena of psychological tests are the stress scales. These scales list life events such as birth, marriage, job promotion, vacation, and so forth and assign each a numerical value which represents the degree of stress thought to be inherent in that event. The sum total of points is assumed to tell individuals how much stress they have in their life. If the subject's score exceeds certain criteria, the subject is advised that he or she is at high risk to experience some sort of mental, emotional, or physical breakdown.

The assumption behind these surveys is that stress is inherent in the events of life, even supposedly positive events such as a move to a new home or a vacation. The more basic underlying assumption, then, is that stress is not only inherent in certain situations, but that it is an unavoidable part of change. The presence or absence of stress is not the question in these surveys—stress is taken as a given and the only variable is how much is present in each event. In essence, these types of tests help foster the belief that life is composed of a continuous series of stressors which threaten not only our well being, but our survival as well. Some people find their tranquility disturbed by a stress test score, which suggests that they are at major risk for a personal catastrophe! The effects of stress surveys are, at best, stressful.

Stress scales were developed from descriptive studies of those events that are stressful for people who are living within the confines of certain conditioned belief systems at a given level of insecurity. The theories used to interpret this test data do not take into account the existence of separate realities or levels of conscious understanding. These theories do not take into account that stress is not inherent in an event, but rather is a result of how an individual *perceives* that event. The proof of this is that many individuals carry out jobs or succeed in situations assumed to have a high degree of stress, and yet these individuals enjoy their work and do not, in fact, experience stress. So, what are we telling people when we tie stress to marriage, parenthood, work, vacation, retirement, and so forth?

PERSONALITY AND PSYCHOPATHOLOGY TESTS

An identical situation exists in the case of the ever-growing list of personality and/or psychopathology tests. All of these tests depend on each other or on some established theory in order to be called "valid." When a person takes these tests, he or she is given labels such as schizophrenic, psychotic, neurotic, feminine, masculine, hypochondriacal, compulsive, and so forth. Yet, every time that we assign a label to a person we are literally conditioning not only the client, but ourselves as therapists, to think of that person in these terms. When such thoughts are accepted by an individual, that person becomes the fulfillment of that label.

This occurs because most people who seek psychological help are insecure and are looking for an expert to tell them who they are and to explain what is happening to them. In this sense, clients are very suggestible to a diagnosis that fits within the framework of what they consider to be their problem. When people are unaware of their own roles in creating problems, they are receptive to any explanation that places the responsibility for their experiences outside the boundaries of their control. Many people who do not know better actually believe that their "personality" is what makes them do what they do. As a result, many of today's psychological tests and the interpretations that are derived from them, make it more difficult for clients to recognize the principles of separate realities in a way that would free them from stress or emotional trauma.

Just as the level of understanding exemplified by the traditional theories has become dependent on techniques to do therapy, so has the present level of understanding become dependent on the use of psychological tests to assess why people are having problems and how to help them. Unfortunately, these tests are based on theories that are not accurate statements of how people function psychologically, what causes problems, or how to help them.

DIAGNOSTIC LABELS: FIXING NEGATIVE PERCEPTION

The study we noted in Chapter 1 in which normal, mentally healthy professionals were admitted as patients to various mental institutions, did not only highlight the inability of mental health staff to recognize sanity, it also exemplified the destructive power of diagnostic labels. Once these "pseudopatients" were diagnosed as being psychotic, every behavior pattern that they exhibited was seen as part of their pathology.

One of the main points made by the psychologist who carried out this innovative study was that, based on our present-day level of thinking, the diagnostic labels that the mental health field bestows on people are, in fact, themselves negative in nature. These labels endure even after people leave the mental health setting. They are not only incorporated into the patient's insecure thinking, but also into the perceptions and expectations of relatives, friends, and society. These labels are eventually accepted by the patients themselves. All of the varied and excessive meanings that these labels carry become the guiding principle for the lives of people who accept them.

In the eyes of society, family, and friends, what can be expected from a person who is schizophrenic or who is supposedly a psychological time bomb because of posttraumatic stress disorder? Do we expect a happy life that includes a beautiful family and a good job, or do we look for abnormal behavior, imminent breakdown, and rehospitalization?

MENTAL ILLNESS AND LEVELS OF CONSCIOUSNESS

Disorganized behavior patterns which can be manifested in the conditions presently labeled functional psychoses (schizophrenia), neuroses (anxiety, phobias), personality disorders, and situation reactions, do exist, but not for the reason given by traditional psychological theories (e.g. past experience, repressed feelings, genetic factors, etc.). All represent the experiences of varying degrees of insecure thoughts, which in turn, create insecure feelings. Feelings of insecurity can take the form of any degree of fear, panic, anger, jealousy, envy, suspiciousness, paranoia, helplessness, and hopelessness. When people are having severe emotional problems, they are caught up in a world of circular negative thinking that is, to some degree, devoid of understanding. Because these disordered realities exist at low levels of understanding about the role that one's own thought plays in the creation of that reality, people attempt to use their disordered thoughts to think their way out of their difficulty. Of course, this solution only makes matters worse.

There is no doubt that there are many people who are in need of guidance. As a field, however, we must begin to take a more compassionate look at the predicament of these people and realize that, due to their troubled states of mind, they are attracted to or actively seek out explanations that fit with their experiences and expectations. Many such people will accept a label and comply with a treatment that appears to be consistent with their perceived troubles, not knowing that at the same time they are accepting more problems.

Every time mental health professionals label patients or tell them that they have certain problems because of certain experiences from their pasts, they are making the situations worse. Imagine what George (Chapter 1) would feel like if he accepted the belief that having sex with his pregnant wife was really hostility toward his unborn child! The human thought system is suggestible to implanting, coding, and programming. People have emotional problems because they think and subsequently perceive and feel that they are predisposed to those problems. People become convinced of being troubled and become confirmed neurotics, paranoids, or whatever the theory and diagnosis happen to be. Each time we categorize people or classify them according to their habitual conditioned patterns and the manifestations of insecurity, we make them prisoners of those realities. Most therapies today are in essence countertherapeutic, because they lead patients away from the realization that they do not have to live at the mercy of conditioned thought patterns. Few are the professionals who can clarify for clients that although they may have serious problems, the solutions are not as serious as the problems.

CHAPTER TWELVE

A Perspective
on Traditional
Psychotherapies

Any psychological theory that directs a human being to link his or her emotional disturbances to anything other than his or her level of consciousness and ability to think has missed the fact that it is just such maladaptive links that are at the core of people's problems. This is because psychological theories originate in thought and, in the absence of an understanding of thought, are as self-validating as any other belief system. As was illustrated in the previous chapter, traditional psychological theories have been constructed at very low levels of understanding thought. As a result these theories invariably link the quality of people's experiences and behaviors to arbitrary external factors, either past or present. In this chapter, we will look at the origin of this tradition and how it has shaped the manner in which psychotherapy is conceived and practiced.

TRADITIONAL PSYCHOTHERAPY: WHAT IT DOES WITH PROBLEMS

Most present-day psychological therapies have been derived from two basic traditions, the psychoanalytical and the behavioristic. The analytically oriented theories were derived from the ideas introduced by Sigmund Freud. The fundamental assumption of this tradition is that human beings are basically controlled by unconscious conflicts and early childhood experiences. This perspective considers the human being to be driven by strong irrational forces which involve sexual and aggressive impulses. Adult problems are considered to be the result of personality flaws that stem from unresolved childhood conflicts such as a man's assumed unresolved sexual desire toward his mother (the Oedipus complex).

The therapies derived from the psychoanalytic tradition involve the analysis and interpretation of the client's dreams, behaviours, recalling and/or reexperiencing past experiences (sometimes as far as the birth experience), analyzing fears, traumas, resistance, as well as the patient's feelings toward the therapist. (The case of George [Chapter 1], provides one example of this type of therapy.) All of these techniques are designed to help the client gain access to the unconscious conflicts that are assumed to be the cause of his or her problems. Psychoanalytic therapy often involves emotional catharsis in which clients are encouraged to express negative emotions on the theory that these emotions have been repressed and stored. Although a great variety and number of combinations of theories exist today, they share a common origin and direction. In fact, many of the founders of subsequent therapies were students of Freud himself or were initially trained in Freudian thinking.

Seemingly, at the the other extreme lie the behavioral therapies. These therapies were constructed on the basis of learning/ conditioning theories derived mostly from animal research. The basic problem associated with these therapies is that they are based on the assumption that a human being's behavior is primarily shaped and controlled by his past and present environment. This view is essentially deterministic in that today's behavior is determined by what happened yesterday. The core idea behind these therapies is that people, like animals, are the products of their environment. Unlike the analytically derived therapies, the behavioral therapies focus exclusively and strictly on observed behavior. However, if one looks deeper, one finds some interesting similarities to the analytical approaches. For example, the behavioral assessment includes the description and the analysis of the present problem, from the perspective of how long, how strong, and how often the undesirable habit manifested itself in the past.

With this information, the behavioral therapist theoretically determines the history of reinforcement as well as the past and present stimuli which contributed to its present elicitation and maintenance of the problematic habits. The treatment may then include using positive, negative, or punishment contingencies to extinguish some habits and/or establish other habits. Again, the case of George provides a good example of a behavioral approach to therapy. Although seemingly different, both the behavioral and the dynamic therapies, then, fall into the same pattern of focusing on, dissecting, analyzing, and justifying people's problems. Both the analytically derived and the behavioral therapies contain a focus on the past (either conditioning or significant events) as being the cause of a behavior pattern that is now locked into the person and out of personal control, requiring the use of some external mechanism (reconditioning, catharsis, analysis) to purge or to alter the behavior. Thus the fundamental assumption underlying both classses of therapy is that the individual is either intrinsically flawed or empty. In either case, this individual has no direct control over his or her life. Any change, therefore, is seen as being achieved only from an outside process.

COGNITIVE THERAPIES: THE TIP OF THE ICEBERG

The cognitive approaches seem to be on the verge of recognizing the Principle of Thought as presented in this book. The basic assumption of the cognitive therapies is that people's perception and feelings are mediated by their beliefs, which are learned patterns of thinking. This is absolutely true. However, the first generation of therapies that have tried to utilize this assumption have not sufficiently understood that thought mediates all beliefs on a moment-to-moment basis. Consequently, when one looks at these first-generation cognitive therapies, it becomes obvious why they do not convey an understanding of thought to the patient. To begin with, all of these therapies are fixated on the content of thought, that is, people's beliefs. There is no recognition that thought content is produced on a moment-to-moment basis by a human being's ability to think, and that the problem is that, ignorant of the fact of thinking, people think that beliefs can possess the thinker! Thus much of cognitive therapies involves monitoring, examining, judging, analyzing, disputing, and in essence fighting beliefs as if beliefs had a life of their own. All sorts of techniques are used to help clients replace faulty software (beliefs) with supposedly better software.

In view of the road that psychotherapy has traveled, there can be no doubt that the cognitive therapies are a step in the right direction. However, in their present form, these therapies are so contaminated with the techniques, rituals, and beliefs carried over from the old traditional therapies, that the necessary ingredient never reaches the client. For example, in order to help people change their beliefs, the traditional cognitive therapist may use techniques such as hypnosis, relaxation, rehearsal, self-monitoring, journal keeping, and self-reinforcement. These techniques and rituals become the focal point of therapy. One must remember that the client experiences these therapies from a reality that may be entirely devoid of knowing about thought, separate realities, feelings, or moods. So, from the context of a patient's reality, what a therapist may be conveying is that the ritual or technique is the source or mediator of mental health. This, of course, is never the case. Only a change in level of consciousness can bring mental health, and this is precisely what an understanding of thought represents.

What is missing from present-day forms of cognitive therapy, then, is the recognition that substituting good beliefs for bad beliefs is not the point. The point is that beliefs are only important when the individual's level of consciousness is devoid of an understanding of thought. So, for example, a client, Scott, may believe that he cannot be happily married to a woman who makes more money than he does. And in a low level of consciousness, where Scott unconsciously uses his thinking to judge and analyze this situation, this will be true. However, if Scott were to have these very same thoughts in a state of mind where he felt love for this same woman, such thoughts, would be laughable. The ideal, of course, would be for Scott to recognize that it was his level of consciousness that determined the quality of his reaction to his own thoughts. Such a recognition would begin to raise his level of understanding of how his thinking is related to what he perceives and feels.

THE PLACEBO EFFECT IN MENTAL HEALTH

All of the previously described forms of therapy depend on the client's belief that a certain technique or ritual will help them. This derives from the fact that these therapies do not consider the client's level of understanding to be the core ingredient in therapeutic psychological change. In view of the principles presented in this book, the results associated with the traditional psychotherapies would be limited to a placebo effect.

The placebo effect is a situation in which a change in personal experience is attributed to some object, ritual, or condition that has no direct relationship to the particular change other than the relationship the individual thinks it has. That is, the actual source of the change is the person's thought about the object, ritual, or condition. So, as was the case with Scott and his thoughts about his wife's income the necessary condition for any placebo to have an effect that the individual must be in a state of consciousness that is devoid of an understanding or an unawareness of thinking. In such a state, the individual's thinking (belief) regarding the relationship of the placebo object to the desired change will, to a significant degree, shape his experience. The more doubtless the thought, the greater the effect.

The effects of a placebo can range from minimal to quite pronounced. The most commonly known situation in which placebos are used is one in which a person wishes relief from some negative condition (pain, anxiety). In such cases, a sugar pill or water injection may be administered as the remedy. The patient is told that he or she is being given medicine that will bring relief. The individual taking treatment has no idea that he or she is taking an inert substance. There are two crucial aspects of this phenomenon. First, the individual believes that the placebo will work. For example, a sugar pill can actually be experienced as reducing or eliminating pain, if the patient thinks that it is an analgesic. Second, because all placebo rituals are connected to an identifiable form (that is, the therapist, the treatment, the techniques, the pill) which has a beginning and an end, the effects are temporary and do not eliminate the problem at its source. A patient involved in such a reality earnestly awaits the next dose of this remedy once the previous dose wears off!

One interesting aspect of the placebo effect is that it can occur regardless of the source of the negative condition. For example, pain relief using a placebo can occur with pain associated with surgical operations as well as with cases where there is no identifiable source of pain. The illusory quality of the placebo effect is not the effect (the change) itself, but rather what is *thought* by the person receiving the placebo.

A Perspective on Traditional Psychotherapies

The Implications of the Placebo Effect

The long-term harmful result of using techniques and rituals to try to guide people out of negative states of mind is that their use perpetuates the level of understanding and the framework of thought which creates such disturbances. The problems that are given power through our thoughts are taken seriously. We attribute our disturbances to some external object (wife, husband, situation) that appears to us to be the cause of emotional reactivity, but that in actuality did not create this condition. The technique, then, does nothing to help the client realize the actual source of mental and/or emotional upset.

Some therapists have asked, what is the harm in a technique that gives someone a nice feeling? The answer to this question is simple. A technique sets the stage for the client to continue to accept a misperception as a fact. First of all, a technique cannot create a feeling. Thought alone has the power to create a feeling. Second, a technique will only create a temporary nice feeling because it leads the client to believe that that technique is necessary for a nice feeling to exist. This would further distract the patient from realizing that it is one's own understanding of *thought* that is the true power underlying positive emotional stability. A technique perpetuates the very illusion that creates the problem to begin with—not knowing where feelings of well-being come from.

An example of this is a patient, who, after engaging in some ritual or technique, experiences some degree of the temporary placebo relief (something that is common to virtually any form of intervention). This patient thinks to himself, "It works." Within the reality of that client, it, the ritual or technique, gets the credit for giving the client mental health. However, that client still has no idea of where his relief really came from or what is responsible for its reemergence. This patient may not know that any novel task that requires the participant to change his normal pattern of thinking will result in some relief. So what will happen is that that patient will go out into the world at the same level of understanding that got him into trouble in the first place. All he has acquired is another false belief. This is why there are many patients who believe they have found a technique or ritual that allows them to have a more stable marriage, but are forced to find other techniques or rituals for stress, child rearing, or alcohol abuse. So, in essence, when the true source of mental health is not recognized, problems always abound. Placebos do nothing to help people realize the power of their thoughts in shaping their reality.

Understanding Versus Placebo Effects

Understanding comes as an individual actually observes how thought becomes reality. The realization of this fact is not an intellectual conceptualization. It is the actual experience of going from one reality to another as a result of a change in one's level of consciousness. This experience involves a realization of some degree of factual understanding.

A realization of a psychological fact is what is commonly referred to as an insight; that is, sight into the fact that we are producing whatever reality we are presently living in. Such an experience takes us from one reality to another. An insight into how one functions psychologically is what takes a person from a reality of problems and negative feelings to one where such problems and feelings do not exist to the same degree by virtue of the fact that they are no longer being produced to the same degree. In the midst of a problem, a person may drop the thought of that particular problem. When this happens, the reality can change to one where the problem no longer exists. A new reality has been realized. If the individual having such an experience realizes how the change in reality is connected to a change in their understanding of the use of thought, he or she is then realizing a higher level of conscious understanding. With this higher level of understanding comes the ability to sustain positive feelings.

With a higher understanding of the thought process, a person becomes free from negative thinking patterns which lead to the feelings of insecurity and thus to mental and/or emotional disturbances. Effective therapy, regardless of its actual form, must always be in the direction of the realization of principles rather than the introduction of techniques or placebos that direct a person's attention to externals as solutions to problems.

PRINCIPLE: GOING BEYOND DETAILS

The true function of a therapist is to point people directly toward their mental health. This can only be done when a therapist knows the difference between principle and details. Principle is what is applicable regardless of the specific details of any situation. Details are the units of confusion that differ from one situation to another. A confused, insecure individual may find it difficult to sustain a good, stable relationship. This individual may be prone to arguing or being defensive. Depression or anxiety may be experienced. In such a case, traditional psychotherapies would dictate that the person focus on, and deal with, the details involved in past relationships, past and present stress, anxiety, assertiveness, and so on.

Working at the deeper level of principle, on the other hand, would mean that a person put aside his or her present frame of reference involving problems with all its accompanying details and begin to realize how to stop generating confusion and insecurity.

It makes no sense to produce a problem on one hand and to try and deal with it on the other. Thought is both the source of the problem and the cure. The cure is to stop producing the problem. The details do not matter. Details are only thought. Any thought, regardless of content, is no more or less than any other thought. The content of thought is a problem only when we forget that it is thought.

Therapy, when focusing on the details of a person's problems, is counterproductive not only because the details are irrelevant, but also because by taking the details seriously, the therapist is actually reinforcing the level of understanding that is behind the perception of the problem. Remember, insecurities compel us to find reasons, justifications, and external solutions to our problems. Therefore, interacting with clients by seriously engaging their level of insecurity is of absolutely no value. A therapy that focuses primarily on reasons, justifications, and external solutions is simply complying with a client's insecurity.

For example, if a woman goes to a therapist because her husband travels on his job more than she likes, and she feels lonely and fearful about their relationship, most therapies would either teach her methods to cope with her loneliness or techniques to get her husband to change his behavior. Yet, there is another alternative. If this client sees the fact that it is simply her own thoughts in a low state of mind that are creating these feelings, then she would realize that the way to get relief is to stop dwelling on insecure thoughts. Her state of mind would then rise to a higher level where she would feel good even if her husband didn't change his job.

SUFFERING AS THERAPY

Many psychological theories postulate that pain and suffering are useful, worthwhile, helpful, or even necessary for growth to take place. As a result, many people feel that it is worthwhile to discuss or "work through" negative feelings and emotions. Many people go to therapists to help them bring out and experience negative feelings, believing that it is healthy to express pain. They think that they have certain feelings "locked inside" of themselves, and this is what is causing their problems.

Thus many traditional therapies encourage people to experience their negative feelings. This is supposed to help angry people get rid of their anger and sad people get rid of their sadness. Yet, as has already been discussed, feelings and emotions are not stored up somewhere in the human body or psyche. Rather, they are created moment to moment through thought and are indicative of our level of consciousness at the time. Thought produces feelings. All that a person has to do to feel angry is to think about something that makes them angry in a level of consciousness where they do not realize that such feelings are signaling a misuse of thought. This is also true of feelings of sorrow, loneliness, fear, guilt, or resentment. Clients who think up some form of negativity from their past and then express it believe that they have done something therapeutic so they literally, at some point, feel better. However, without an understanding that the relief experienced from catharsis is merely a result of the fact that they have stopped it, clients will never come to the end of the process. In fact, the most common result of getting clients to express negative feelings is that clients learn to generate and express negative feelings.

Such was the case of John, a Vietnam veteran who had been in therapy for four years as a result of depression, anxiety, and guilt over things he had seen and done during his tour of duty. John's lack of understanding of feelings had crippled his ability to be happy. Every time he felt any degree of happiness, John would immediately begin recalling Vietnam experiences. Most of the time, he would go through several days of mental anguish, remembering and knowing that no one else could ever understand what he had done. For years, John had been told by every therapist he had seen that the only way for him to get relief was to recall, relive, and talk about his experiences, get in touch with his feelings, and get them out of his system. John initially fought this logic. To him, that was his problem in the first place. He was already recalling, reliving, and very much in touch with his feelings. But, for lack of knowing any better, John complied.

When John was initially seen by one of the authors, he had recalled, relived, and been in touch with his bad feelings hundreds of times. John did not know the answer, but after four years of fruitless suffering in therapy, there was no doubt in his mind that negativity was not it. John's response to hearing common sense was almost instant. In his second session John related that he had felt a great deal of relief following the first session, but still felt uneasy about getting his hopes up, fearing that he would be "setting himself up for an ambush." By the end of the thirteenth session, John was crying for joy at realizing that his relief was real, that the horrible feelings he had been experiencing were not coming from the past or from a flaw in his mind, but from his lack of understanding of his present thinking. He realized that his real problem was that his understanding of why he had done certain things had not changed. It did not take him long to see that what he had done in Vietnam was as inhumane as it was innocent. He realized that, given his state of understanding at the time, what he did was understandable. John no longer sees his Vietnam experiences as a curse, but as a very profound lesson. John once said, "I may not be a psychologist or a psychiatrist, but I can assure you I have seen separate realities and levels of consciousness."

Clients come to therapy to find positive states of mind where they will be able to enjoy life. Such states are not found by dwelling on the negativity produced in lower levels of consciousness where people are blind to their own functioning. To help clients eliminate negativity by asking them to entertain negative emotional states is to direct them toward lower states of consciousness in which they utilize their thought systems to create more emotional distress.

Therapists should never encourage patients to pursue the negative. Instead, they should guide their clients toward realizing the fact that thought creates feelings because in order to eliminate negative feelings, people must first realize their source. Clients must realize for themselves the principles that underly their ability to feel emotions, which, when understood, will lead them away from suffering toward the quality of life they are seeking. In any case, the therapist should never forget that the goal of therapy is to guide people out of negative states, away from negative feelings.

WHAT IS MISSING?

What is needed today in the field of mental health is a clearer picture of the relationship of thought, feeling, perception, and behavior instead of therapies that explain one event in terms of another. Then people can free themselves from all their conditioned reactions with neither a need to go back into the past to see where these patterns started, nor a need to reexperience them, express their feelings about them, act them out, or do anything with them. All a person has to do in order to free himself or herself from conditioned thinking and the problems it created is to see that it originates as the voluntary function of thought.

It is not necessarily that the specific goals of any therapy are right or wrong. Rather, we are simply pointing out how the very essence of any method or technique directs people to accept the fundamental assumptions of whatever theory they are associated with. Thus, although there are hundreds of theories and therapies that differ totally in content and detail, all are the same with respect to their fundamental assumptions.

All present-day psychological theories, directly or indirectly, convey a passive view of human potential to people. All assume that the way people behave now is either determined by such things as innate psychic flaws, their birth order or by their pasts. All contemporary theories view mental health as an exception to the rule, something that is out of people's direct control and something that is subject to change only by some outside manipulation done to the clients by the therapists, which often must be constantly repeated over long periods of time for it to have any effect at all. Thus far, no one has been able to demonstrate that any therapy is better than a placebo.[1]

Ironically, it is the insecurity associated with our ability to get the results desired that weds us as professionals to our techniques, irrespective of theoretical orientation. We are known as the experts and therefore feel that we want to do something to help people. What we fail to realize is that the very doing of that something is in itself making it harder for us to really help people. Techniques create a barrier to giving people a deeper common sense about what they are doing themselves, to create and maintain the unique versions of reality in which they live and experience all of their problems.

CHAPTER THIRTEEN

Application of Psychological Principles to Organizations

Previously, we discussed how the principles of human psychological functioning can be applied to therapy and counseling. Our experiences have shown that these principles not only provide a new direction for mental health professionals, but are also directly applicable to the field of organizational psychology.

The primary principle that has become increasingly clear to us in our work as consultants is that human psychological functioning (and dysfunctioning) is not restricted to nonworking hours. We have recognized the link between employees', including managers', overall level of mental health and their ability to do their job well. There is no doubt that the "normative" breakdowns in employees' mental health adversely affect such things as productivity, motivation, judgment, and job satisfaction. In fact, we believe that employees' mental health is the most valuable asset of any organization.

THE TRADITION

In an effort to create more effective organizations, management theory has borrowed from a variety of traditional psychological models. These models have spawned countless techniques to promote organizational decision making, problem solving, communication skills, stress management, group dynamics, motivation, and productivity. Although such developments are a step in the right direction because they attempt to improve the system, management programs based on these models and techniques have failed to bring about the long-term resolution of organizational problems. The main reason for this failure is that, as discussed in Chapter 12, the use of techniques as a means of overcoming or eliminating malproductive behavior has the effect of directing people's awareness toward the techniques and away from the real source of lasting change—their level of consciousness—leaving them with what is known as a placebo effect. For example, a classic study investigated the effect of various working conditions on rate of output at the Western Electric Company's Hawthorne plant.[1] After a year of measuring worker productivity, the study found that, regardless of the change that was instituted (which involved different configurations of rest periods and longer or shorter days), each change resulted in a temporarily higher rate of work than usual. In other words, these temporary results came about not because of the specific change that was made, but because the workers felt they were special, they were in an interesting experiment, and they knew that their production rate was being measured. This study noted that the workers were happy and they complied with the desires of the experimenter. Again, the reader will see the similarity between what happened in this study and those cited in Chapter 10 (showing the willingness of subjects to comply with the wishes of the experimenter). The Hawthorne study has become such a classic in the field, that the placebo effect in the realm of business and management consulting has come to be known as the "Hawthorne effect."

So, as was the case in helping the individual realize a better quality of life, techniques alone can never bring lasting change or relief in an organization because a technique is an attempt to create or re-create a certain effect *in the absence of psychological understanding.* In the absence of a deeper understanding of the real source of the change, the effects of motivational or job-enhancement programs are always temporary. In the absence of an understanding of levels of consciousness, situations and events will continue to occur in ways that trigger employees' insecurities, thereby adversely affecting their performance.

PSYCHOLOGY AND THE WORKPLACE

What people in charge of organizations are in need of is a more universal psychological understanding of people that gives them an increased perspective from which to work with employees in ways that maximize potential and minimize stress and ineffectiveness. Such an understanding allows managers and supervisors to see, moment to moment, what is actually causing employees (or themselves) to lose sight of the source of their motivation, enthusiasm, and desire to do a good job, and what to do to restore effective functioning. Up until recently, such an approach has not been available.

ORGANIZATIONAL REALITIES

Things go wrong when people in an organization have no idea what is happening to them and other people at a psychological level in terms of how their moods and feelings about work change. This is understandable. Organizations are comprised of a mix of people, a mix of separate realities. Each of these people comes to work with a unique psychological frame of reference. They come to work with individualized expectations, biases, prejudices, beliefs and feelings about who they are, how other people see them, how they should be treated as well as a fixed notion of what certain behaviors mean. They come to work at various levels of consciousness, and during the day they fluctuate through mood levels, positive and negative, without realizing that this is happening. So it is in this state that people organize together for the express purpose of helping the sick, teaching the young, or producing a product.

In an organization, whether it is a school system, public agency, or private business, the bulk of problems arise when the members

219

of that organization experience a drop in their level of mental health. As was noted in Chapter 4, normal people experience daily fluctuations in their level of mental health. Normal people do, in fact, have periods of time when their mood level drops into the low range of psychological functioning and they feel upset, depressed, angry, used, and mistreated. People in these states over-react to things that they would handle in stride if they were feeling better and often disregard things to which they would otherwise appropriately respond.

Workers in low mood levels, whether induced by personal problems or organizational pressure and inequities, are inefficient, un-motivated, and accident prone. If this low level becomes a chronic condition, workers may experience problems with co-workers, may have excessive absenteeism, or even turn to alcoholism and drug abuse. The organization may experience these problems in the form of a high employee turnover rate. In reality these things are symptomatic of an employee level of mental health that has dropped low enough to be called dysfunctional. Unfortunately, if this situation is not recognized for what it is—a temporary dip in psychological functioning—the dysfunctioning can be passed on from one person to another, in the guise of an organizational issue or through commiseration, until a pervasive state of low morale exists. At this point you have groups of people who are reactive, defensive, and fighting for control. Communication breaks down, procedures are overlooked, cooperation ceases, and productivity falls. People become fixated with the *details* of what is going wrong but fail to recognize the *reason* that things are going downhill. It is not recognized that the level of mental health or common sense has dropped low enough to render the people ineffective.

One such situation was exemplified in the findings surrounding the 1986 Space Shuttle Challenger disaster. It has been discovered that there was a wealth of technical experts who had repeatedly warned the agency of the high probability of a malfunction of the solid rocket booster O-ring seals, as well as the dire outcome of such a malfunction. These warnings were specific, precise, detailed, and so numerous that it is difficult for people to comprehend how they possibly could have been ignored. The answer to this riddle lies in understanding what insecurity does to people, their feelings, perceptions, and judgments at an organizational level. As was documented by the investigation, the space program had been plagued by insecurity deriving from the question of future funding, the threat of cutbacks, loss of jobs, national prestige, and self-image. In this environment, it was next to impossible for these decision makers to listen to the logic and validity of the warnings. Consequently, the perceived urgent pressure to defend its self image outweighed common sense, with unanticipated tragic consequences. This was indirectly noted in the media, but not fully understood in terms of its universal psychological significance.

The ability to function with higher levels of common sense will stabilize an organization when individuals realize that their feelings and perceptions about their work are directly related to what they are thinking in a certain mood level. With this understanding, people realize that negative feelings do not result solely from the work environment, but from what they think or interpret about what is happening and about the significance of that happening. If the individual is not aware that it is his or her thinking that is shaping personal reality, that person will attribute perceptions, good or bad, to the workplace. When this is the case, the individual who is feeling negative will react negatively to the environment as the source of the problem. Such a state of psychological functioning will adversely affect motivation, productivity, communication, initiative, creativity, and overall morale.

Until now, consultants have focused on the effects of people working together in low levels of understanding psychological functioning. This is understandable, because the thinking has been that normal people do not experience changes in their level of mental health to the degree that it would change their view of reality. However, as we know from personal experience, there are times when we all lose our common sense and say and do things that we would never do if we were feeling better. It is extremely beneficial to an organization for management to recognize this fact and how it is connected to the interactions that comprise organizational behaviors.

When this is realized, managers, supervisors, and administrators do not spend all of their time and other valuable resources addressing the symptoms rather than the actual causes. They do not teach a person techniques for stress, communication, decision making, or creativity, only to have that technique break down the moment that that individual's mood drops to a lower level of functioning. Rather, understanding what mental health really is, that manager or administrator knows how to handle problems in a manner that directs the employee toward a higher level of understanding, unobstructed by the form that problem may have taken.

For example, when a school principal talks to teachers who are having a conflict, that administrator discovers that each teacher tells a consistent story about how the other person was wrong. Furthermore, each teacher involved in this conflict will have substantiations to prove his or her point. If the principal does not understand that the teachers are reporting, to the best that their level of understanding allows, what seems true to them, then this principal will not realize that these teachers' separate realities are clashing with each other in low levels of functioning. If this crucial point is overlooked, the administrator will become confused, the issue will get clouded, and the intervention may well create increased friction and misunderstanding. Yet when these disturbed teachers are given a chance to calm down and regain their positivity (mental health), their differences in perception will be much less important and ways of cooperating will become obvious.

Incredible confusion can result when a supervisor attempts to solve problems by using his or her own separate frame of reference to decide who is right, who is wrong, who is telling the truth, and who is not. The fact is that in separate realities, everyone is right and everyone is telling the truth as they see it. Fault is not the primary issue. To continually find fault and place blame on an individual or a department is counterproductive, if the real issue, which is separate beliefs, separate perceptions, separate interpretations of the same situation made by people in separate mood levels is not addressed. When managers can actually get a glimpse into the fact that these separate realities do, in fact, exist and that they are very much in evidence in the workplace, then they can provide the necessary guidance and education for their employees that allows them to begin to function at a higher level of understanding. Confusion and insecurity tend to disappear when the people in charge know the essence of what underlies harmony and cooperation.

THE RESULT OF INSECURITY IN ORGANIZATIONS

One of the things that helps a manager tremendously is when he or she learns to recognize the psychological condition called insecurity. In any organization, people have their own ways of approaching problems, situations, and other people (i.e., they live in a separate reality). When people feel more insecure than usual, when they are in a lower mood or a lower level of consciousness, these conditioned or habitual ways of doing things become even more important to them. It is at these levels of functioning that people attempt to impose their ideas and beliefs on the people around them. Insecurity, as a form of thinking, leads people to cling to or recall incidents in which they felt that they were wronged. In these states of mind, people revive resentments and negative attitudes toward themselves, other people, and their work. The satisfying, pleasurable feelings of work are replaced with resistance, with unwillingness to cooperate, to provide assistance or expertise when needed. If management attempts to change these views at the same basic level of understanding, an atmosphere of insecurity, a we–they or an I–you opposition can develop between people, departments, or levels of management.

Here again we have the same situation that was depicted in figure 9 on page 155 of Chapter 9, as it related to change in therapy. What is interesting is that, in the organizational setting, although the context and details have changed, the basic principles of what happens when people become entrenched in their own views of reality remains the same.

This kind of situation is symptomatic of insecurity. When people in an organization become insecure, that feeling filters and distorts their perceptions and their approaches to problems, their relationships with others, their ability to listen, their level of creativity and motivation. In any organization, conflicts between management and staff, between co-workers or between departments can be traced back to the low-mood feeling of insecurity. Negativity is as detrimental to the smooth running of an organization as friction is to the smooth running of an engine.

Managers who are feeling insecure and who do not know what this feeling means and how it is produced, will focus on some form of self-protection. They will be on the lookout for trouble. They will talk down to employees, have an elevated idea of their own importance, and guard this image of self-importance with their lives. They will be reluctant to admit mistakes and will tend to blame problems on someone or something else. They will not look to themselves to discover their role in the problem. They will overlook the fact that, as organizational leaders, they have knowingly or unknowingly contributed to whatever situation exists. When there is difficulty in an organization, the person at the top is ultimately responsible, but if that person is insecure, he or she will place blame elsewhere instead of looking for a clearer, more secure and objective state of mind as a guide to resolving the problem.

ALAN: A CASE STUDY *

Alan was a 53-year-old vice president for a manufacturing company in which the management approach derived from the Psychology of Mind was applied. He was a 27-year man in the organization; having started as a production engineer at the age of 26, he had done very well for himself. He had made a change to line management at 31, becoming a supervisor in a heavy manufacturing setting, and by 38, had been made plant manager. At the very young age of 44, he was made general manager of his company, one of the youngest in the corporation. For the past three years he had been vice president of the manufacturing division. The division was comprised of three manufacturing companies. The largest, from which Alan had come, provided research and development, engineering, and sales support for all three and employed nearly 300 people. The remaining two were satellite manufacturing facilities, each with about 100 employees. These companies had a history, particularly in the last seven or eight years, of high employee turnover, absenteeism, and even some more serious chemical dependency problems with employees. As Alan was tak-

* The authors are indebted to the staff of Vantage Consulting, Inc., for providing this individual case study.

ing over the vice president's chair, increased competition due to technological change was creating new problems and highlighting old ones. Quality control problems were increasing. For example, rework (having to redo a product after production) was eating holes in the bottom line, and everyone was scrambling to adjust to computerization and mechanization of the manufacturing process in order to remain competitive.

Alan's personal level of commitment to the company had always been high. His beliefs about people and work, however, did not allow this commitment to translate into an ability to manage. The following quote characterized Alan's method of managing employees: "There are very few people you can really trust to do a job, so give these people all they can take. Use pressure and authority as best you can to get the rest of the people to do the remainder of the work. Very few of that remainder will rise to the top and, as for the rest, people are people, basically weak, and we have no choice but to let the chips fall where they may and do the best we can." So, although Alan was occasionally enthusiastic about a highly committed and motivated "bright star" he saw rising through the ranks, he perceived more than enough game playing, politics, and insecurity going on in the environment to overshadow his enthusiasm and motivation.

Working with Alan was a challenge because he was not a big fan of management and motivational theory. Throughout his career in various positions, he had felt obliged to attend many seminars and extended training programs that dealt with interpersonal skills, team building, decision making, motivation, and so forth. Early on, such topics had been of great interest to him and he had earnestly tried to apply some of the many techniques offered. Some techniques had seemed to help, but only for a while, and then it was back to the all too familiar patterns.

Shortly after orienting upper level management, we completed our interview process (talking to over 75% of the people in this organization), produced our report, and presented it to management. In Alan's own words, there were no surprises. "We already knew that some divisions were not doing a good job of initial employee training and that safety sometimes takes a back seat to production priorities. There will always be supervisors who resort to intimidation with employees." He knew, too, from his own experience, that there was a natural fear of "Corporate Headquarters" and the executive branch. What he didn't fully acknowledge was the degree to which we saw this fear as paralyzing relations and, therefore, limiting and distorting crucial management information and perceptions.

The first order of business for Alan was to begin to understand responsibility and the impact of one's own state of mind on the organization. We spoke about "mental clarity" as a state that could be achieved by understanding the principles of our own mental functioning. This state of mind was described as a vantage place, where, from a quieter, less judgmental frame of reference, we could look with understanding at others and the organization and see where and how we could help. This state or vantage place created a psychological shift into what could be described as a "state of service." At this point we could see that Alan was bristling a little: "I do consider things well and I've always been willing to help anyone with the guts to ask!"

Alan recognized that fear was present in the environment, but saw it essentially as a "very necessary evil" or even as a motivational tool. "How else could we get things done? A little stress is healthy. Those who succeed, do so because they can handle it, 'rally to the cause' and rise to the top despite or because of their fear. Pressure separates the wheat from the chaff." We listened to Alan and didn't try to push our point. However, we asked Alan to keep an open mind about the effects of fear in the environment and management's role in creating it and becoming dependent on it.

About this time, Alan was becoming curious about the program. We had outlined psychological principles. We had, in his view, presented an accurate (if not a little strong) view of the organization and its human relations climate, but we had yet to offer any new technique or advice (other than generalities) to deal with the situation. When we replied that we would not offer him any psychological techniques, he was perplexed. He listened to our explanation about techniques being of limited value because one's actual depth of understanding did not shift or deepen. He could see this on an intellectual level, but the "program" was still a mystery to him.

However, Alan was changing. Later we were to find out that he was beginning to see some things about his personal state of mind, not as it related to work, but at home, with his wife and three teenage children. He had begun to watch his relationships with these people and to see how he set up and contributed to negativity and insecurity. He was beginning to bite his tongue and watch with understanding instead of jumping head first into situations. He found himself wanting to do something nice with his children instead of getting on their cases. When his wife was in an off mood, or if she was complaining about something, he was finding he would rather fix her a cup of tea than argue. Home was becoming more peaceful. Now, if he could only make it happen at work.

One thing that was consistent in Alan's case was that almost everyone who worked for him was in fear of him. Some simply saw him as firm and demanding, others saw him as aggressive and manipulative. Several people recounted stories of how employees would suddenly have business out of the office or field work to do when Alan came around. He often found closed doors and people on long phone calls when he was on the premises. These views were consistently held from person to person, department to department, and from one division to another. On the positive side, in what appears to be a contradiction, were a number of volunteered accounts by employees and supervisors (levels that did not report directly to Alan) praising his kindness, consideration of older employees, and in fact, his amazing ability to know great numbers of employees on a first-name basis.

Alan was shocked and somewhat hurt as we showed him how he was perceived by his midmanagement team. He felt that, even though we saw these reports as "perceptions" and didn't take any one as gospel, we were coloring things too darkly. "Surely I would be more aware of it if things were that bad," he said. We reminded Alan of one of our group sessions in which we pointed out that everyone has some degree of insecurity and that in the workplace, such insecurity is typically associated with the authority of those above them. Fear of people who are in control and have the power to end our source of income is understandable. With this fear, employees would frequently misinterpret the behavior of managers. Alan listened.

We advised him to change the tone of his next few visits to his staff. We asked him to keep the principles we had taught him in the back of his mind and observe what happened. "Watch particularly for the presence of fear when meeting with people. If you see it, don't judge it, just try to put the person at ease. With people whose nervousness is more blatant, change your pattern—have lunch with them, talk about areas in which they are confident and have done well. Get to know them again, as people rather than workers. Above all else, observe your own thoughts and the feelings that come as a result."

We asked Alan to drop his past history with people as much as he could, and see them as if he were meeting them for the first time. Alan promised to follow our advice as best he could over the next month. We warned him not to expect too much too fast, but to keep an open mind.

The Other Side of the Fence

A consultant who attempts to help in any relationship must be aware of one cardinal rule at all times: "It takes two to tango." In Alan's case, there were two or three managers whose reaction to him was extreme and who had a particularly hard time working for him.

One manager, Len, had been the quality control manager at one of Alan's companies for just over three months. During the interview process, he said he was quite nervous around Alan. He cited a couple of occasions when Alan had "called him on the carpet" and, from his perspective, he felt he was not given an opportunity to defend or explain himself.

Len claimed he came into the job with a positive attitude toward Alan, saying that as an employee and later as a supervisor, Alan had always treated him respectfully and considerately. He noted, in fact, that as an employee, he had observed that Alan was one of the few "higher ups" who would take the time to come around and thank people for a "job well done."

As Len moved up into management ranks, he began to hear some negative stories about Alan, and after he had had a few trying experiences with him personally, he found himself joining lunchtime commiseration sessions in which he and other managers swapped war stories about their encounters with corporate executives. Before Len realized what was happening, he had joined the we–they mentality that existed between his company's management team and corporate executives.

During our sessions at the company, we talked about how per-

230

ceptions develop and are hardened. We talked about how individuals and even groups of individuals hold each other in the past. During one session, we discussed the subject of responsibility and of how our own insecurities and thoughts can make a situation or relationship seem worse than it is. Len was very interested in this and stayed even after the session was over for more discussion. He wanted to know, from what we had observed, if his relationship with Alan was a case in point. Our answer was a definite yes. Len quickly pointed out those occasions when he did feel Alan had been hard on him. We let him know that that may be true, but in retrospect it would be hard to tell how much Alan contributed to the situation and how much of the problem was Len's own fear interpreting those encounters.

The facts were that Len was working indirectly for Alan and had the choice either to remain in this negative pattern, or to make an honest effort to change this reality. We assured Len that Alan, too, was looking at his own perceptions and behavior and deserved a second chance. Len was fascinated now and actually excited about the possibility of seeing things differently.

A New Experience

All this was happening as Alan made his rounds, trying his best to follow our counsel. He was beginning to see signs of change at work as he had at home. As Alan told us later, it was about his third visit with Len since Alan started making his new effort, when something caught his eye. He had gone out of his way not to put Len on the spot in his previous two visits and had purposely steered clear of a couple of touchy items he was concerned about. As he did so, he began to see a different side of Len. Alan saw a man with a sense of humor and an honest concern about his job and his employees. Alan said he remembers thinking to himself, "Why haven't I seen this in Len before?"

During his third visit, Alan found Len in a great mood, very receptive and up. He seemed genuinely glad to see Alan. The interaction was going great as Len brought Alan up to date on things and informed him of future plans. During this process, how-ever, Len appeared to gloss over an area of concern that Alan had, regarding computerization plans for his department. Alan needed to know how Len was progressing in this area, so he asked about it again. Instantly, Alan saw Len's face and demeanor change from good humor to insecurity. Alan began to feel disappointment creeping in on him as he watched this young manager fidget.

Then suddenly, Len stopped in midsentence, turned, and looked Alan in the eye and said, "No, that's all bullshit. The truth is I've fallen behind. I don't really understand what I'm supposed to at this point in the computerization program. Our manual sys-tems are different from the other companies, and we're scrambling to get them converted and caught up. I need some extra help here."

Alan was genuinely moved by Len's courage and honesty and, at the same time, happy to have a handle on what the real situation was. "Don't worry about it, Len, everyone's having problems with this program in one way or another. I'll get you some help and extra training from the home office. I'll come out and work with you as well, because I need a little better understanding of what we're up against myself."

When Len told us his side of this story, he brought it to the point where things were breaking down in the meeting, and he said, "*I saw it.* I saw fear coming in and taking over and then I saw that it had nothing to do with Alan. In fact, he was being very supportive. I knew it was me, so I pulled myself together and was as honest as I could be. Alan's response was amazing—nothing but support; no recriminations, just help. I felt tremendous relief, a real freedom. I've never gone home from work feeling so clear and encouraged."

Now, after a number of similar experiences and the resulting increase in organizational effectiveness (including "the bottom-line"), Alan is an enthusiastic supporter of the program. He tells us that he now has employee relationships he can count on. He feels he has access to real management information, uncluttered by evasiveness and politics. More important, he sees people differently, because he sees himself differently. Alan can see now when he is in a "state of service" to others and where he can help.

A year after these events began to occur, Alan told a group of managers in one of our training sessions, "This has been the best year of my career. I know what's going on in my companies, our programs and plans are getting into place much more easily, and I'm enjoying work so much more. I never would have believed that it was me that had to change for all this to happen."

This story is not meant to insinuate that a panacea exists which will cure every working relationship and turn every manager or employee into an excellent performer. What we are saying is that a deeper level of understanding or vantage place exists from which the maze of interpersonal relationships in organizations can be seen more clearly and can, therefore, be managed much more productively.

As managers get into a "state of service" to those who report to them, respect increases and honest dialogue begins. Many managers have, at first, mistaken the "state of service" as a "soft stance"—a leniency toward poor performance or unacceptable behavior. On the contrary, this position provides the clarity for supervisors and managers to see their own contributions to a negative pattern and, in effect, removes excuses. Help can then be offered honestly and accountability can be expected, within the context of fairness and understanding. When supervisors are able to shift into this perspective with employees, then the same process of understanding and mutual respect is initiated.

This shift in perspective is illustrated in figure 8 (8B to 8A), page 145 of Chapter 9. From this vantage point, managers can see when employees are exhibiting poor performance as a result of their insecurity. Such a perspective allows managers to manage those employees in a way that will maximize the likelihood of helping them rise out of their insecure frame of reference, to realize a more positive motivational and productive state.

Once again, the beauty of the principles of the Psychology of Mind is that they provide a common denominator for understanding how to foster positive psychological change across separate realities. Whether we are talking about "normal" people, such as Alan, who was experiencing the problems associated with low morale in organizational settings or people such as Olga (in Chapter 9), who was exhibiting a more severe form of psychological disturbance in a clinical setting, the principles underlying their change in perspective remain constant. What becomes clear is that there is a great deal more potential within our human resources, and that the set of principles that comprise the Psychology of Mind represents the most promising tool yet for realizing this potential.

MOTIVATION AND PRODUCTIVITY

When people first come to work for an organization, they usually begin with a positive attitude. They are excited about making a fresh start, enthusiastic about learning new skills and contributing the best they have to offer. In other words, people generally start work with a natural predisposition to function in a higher level of consciousness. This higher frame of reference is the natural source of motivation as was discussed in Chapter 7 and illustrated in figure 5. In this state of mind, there is an absence of insecurity about the workplace. This initial predisposition can be built on to produce highly motivated employees. Such a climate will in turn result in a highly efficient and productive organization in which people truly enjoy working together while supporting and learning from one another.

Alan's change is representative of the type of shift that we have been discussing in this book. That is, Alan did not learn to manage the type of people he perceived to be working for him. No, Alan's change was much deeper than that. Alan changed to the degree that he realized that his employees were not as he had formerly perceived them to be—unmanageable. What Alan saw, from his newfound understanding, were employees who were easily and rewardingly manageable. Human relations management only indirectly manages peoples' behavior. The essence of human relations management is understanding how employee states of mind are affected by different factors in the workplace, including management's own perspective of its employees.

The authors know managers who, like Alan, develop a common-sense understanding of the principles of human psychological functioning so that they are able to maintain a high degree of security, in themselves and in their organization. They accept a high degree of responsibility for what is going on in the organization. These people treat their employees with respect and consideration, seek ideas, and look for ways to help them do their jobs more easily and efficiently. They have the good sense to use the skills, talents, and resources of other people. These people have employees who are loyal, who enjoy coming to work, and who find ways to make their jobs more productive. Such managers are motivated by their own positive feelings, clear vision, enthusiasm, and optimism. A manager with an understanding of how insecurity is produced and maintained in an organization is able to lead people to new levels of cooperation, productivity, and work enjoyment.

The whole point is to awaken in managers a practical understanding that, while employees and managers have separate and unique views of the organization, they may not know this fact or how it affects their perceptions of reality. Every employee goes up and down mood levels, and in low moods everything in that separate reality will look bleak and difficult; in higher moods these same things will look brighter and easier. Managers who understand moods will not focus primarily on the details that people perceive as important in lower levels of functioning, but will focus on guiding employees to higher states of mind where their perception will change for the better. These supervisors and administrators will realize that people do their best when they feel their best, so they will not attempt to motivate by instilling fear or heavy-handed control measures. Instead, they will see common-sense, practical ways to guide people to the natural motivation present in higher moods, higher states of mind. As the mood (morale) of the organization rises, so will the level of mutual respect, cooperation, and creativity. Productivity will increase as stress and burnout diminish or disappear altogether.

Lasting positive changes occur in an organization when administrators, managers, and supervisors begin to see the principles of human functioning behind the details of people's behavior. This understanding automatically gives them the common sense perspective they need to help people become involved in and excited about their work, to give them a good feeling about themselves, their co-workers, and their work that leads to an overall positive contribution to the organization. Using their own common-sense understanding of the basic principles of human psychological functioning, management sets the tone or the level of consciousness that filters down throughout the organization. Gradually, the typical spiral of dissent, defensiveness, misunderstanding, and stress (similar to the cycle of mental disorder illustrated in figure 4, page 64) is replaced by an upward spiral of positive feelings, perceptions, and productive behaviors (also illustrated in figure 4). Management can then free themselves from day-to-day problem solving to carry out more long-range planning and organizational development functions. As the time and energy to develop the organization is increased, the long-run viability of the organization is increased, furthering productivity and work enjoyment. Thus many farsighted organizations have instituted programs that work not just to treat employee (including upper management) mental health dysfunctions that would not have been considered job-related a decade ago, but to enhance their employees' functioning and performance, by raising the level of the entire team's mental health.

CHAPTER FOURTEEN

Mental
Health
in Health
Care

"This woman is demanding, manipulative, and uncooperative. She keeps asking to go to the bathroom, sometimes three times in an hour. She is rude and has upset the staff. If she cannot be more cooperative, we feel that she should be dicharged." This is how a nurse angrily described a 60-year-old woman named Mary whose case was being reviewed at a weekly staff meeting at a rehabilitation unit of a large private hospital. Six weeks prior to this, Mary had been a happy woman who could walk, talk, understand language, and who enjoyed playing with her grandchildren and going fishing with her retired husband. Then suddenly, she had a stroke, which left the right side of her body paralyzed. She lost the ability to speak and, to some extent, to understand the spoken and written word, and she was unable to take care of her hygenic needs. In this state, she was placed in a hospital where she was surrounded by unfamiliar people and routines.

Upon hearing the nursing summary of Mary's progress, several rehabilitation therapists suggested that Mary might be in need of a more reassuring approach. They noted that in their work with Mary they utilized such an approach and found that after 15 to 20 minutes, her mood would usually elevate at which point they were able to successfully involve her in rehabilitation therapies. The nurse did not hear what the therapists were saying. She did not hear this comment as an answer to this nursing dilemma, which it was. Instead, this nurse, from her insecure separate reality, heard something else, something threatening that prompted her to respond in an insecure manner toward the other staff members, saying that if they wanted to take over the nursing responsibilities for this woman they could, and then they could handle this woman in whatever manner they wished.

It was at this point that one of the authors was requested to evaluate Mary in order to find out what her problem was and, perhaps, counsel her so that she would be more compliant with the nursing staff. The findings were indeed revealing. Just prior to one evaluation session, a nurse was observed in the process of cleaning Mary, as she had had a bowel movement in her bed. "What a gross mess. Couldn't you wait another minute? This is disgusting," said the nurse. This nurse had come to work, as many others on this unit often did, with a negative outlook. What this nurse, in her haste and low state of mind, could not see was the stream of tears flowing out of a very silent Mary.

Mary was lucky. She eventually recovered most of her functioning to the degree that she was able to return home and pick up where she left off. Unfortunately, however, Mary's experience in the hospital was typical for this particular unit. When the pervasiveness of this negative situation was described to the unit directors (in the gentlest manner possible), the response was defensiveness and hostility. The solution to this unit's problems could have been as simple as educating the staff regarding what mental health is and how it manifests itelf in our daily lives, along with setting some common sense guidelines in terms of how patients are treated. This particular group, however, was not willing to consider that they or their staff had anything to do with their patient's reactive behavior. They preferred to think that their situation was the result of noncompliant or mentally unstable patients.

The predicament of the nursing staff in relation to Mary is depicted in figure 9, page 155 of Chapter 9. Both the nursing staff and Mary were viewing one another through the filters of their respective insecure levels of consciousness. The level of consciousness of the nursing staff, however, did not allow them to see that Mary was understandably upset given her sudden disability, caught up in an insecure cycle of thinking. The nurses' insecurity also kept them from being able to hear the solution offered by the rehabilitation therapists. In essence, what these therapists were describing was the way to raise Mary's level of consciousness to a level where she experienced more hope and increased motivation to help herself. (As illustrated in figure 8 on page 145 of Chapter 9).

THE HEALTH OF THE HELPER

As was the case with helping individuals with their mental health problems, an understanding of the principles of the Psychology of Mind has provided us with a fresh view of what produces barriers to successful organizational functioning in hospital settings. This new perspective involves a basic understanding of what a hospital is.

A hospital is a place where people who cannot help themselves with a physical or mental problem go to get help from other human beings. People go to hospitals on the assumption that the people who work there will offer the assistance necessary for patients to regain some degree of health. This is not an unreasonable assumption. There is no doubt that physical medicine has evolved to the point that it can offer some degree of help for virtually any ailment. In some cases, it is possible to resolve physical problems that a century ago were considered incurable. In those cases in which a solution has not yet been found, it is possible to help people alleviate some degree of pain and suffering. But one need only spend a brief time in a hospital to realize that there is a great deal of needless suffering being doled out along with the medicine.

One clear example is the case of Cathy. Cathy was a 15-year-old girl who had undergone surgery in order to correct a curvature in her lower back. In the course of her surgery, two steel rods (Herrington rods) had been anchored to the vertebral processes as a means of correcting and stabilizing the curvature. These rods were inserted through an 18-inch incision. Two days after her surgery, Cathy was understandably still experiencing a great deal of pain and requested the pain medication that had been ordered by her doctor. The nurse who was in charge of Cathy's case was not in a very good mood that evening. She felt tired, hurried, and dissatisfied with her job. When Cathy began pushing her call button, this nurse decided to take her time, so as not to be "manipulated" by the patient. When the nurse finally came into the room, her first question to Cathy was an abrupt, "What do you need?" "My pain medicine," answered Cathy. "Where does it hurt?" retorted the nurse. When Cathy answered, "I had back surgery two days ago," this nurse blurted out, "I wonder what other drugs you like." Why have stories such as this become commonplace in our hospitals?

The reason for this ironic situation is that, although health care professionals may have the intellectual and physical skills necessary to help others, they do not always have the necessary mental health to successfully accomplish what they know how to do. Up until recently, no one has clearly recognized that technical skills are manifested through the state of mind of the helper. Thus, in a low level of mental health, staff may not only be unable to carry out their duties, but they will experience their work as a source of stress and negativity. The end result is that they may be spreading confusion and discomfort to patients and co-workers in the course of their interactions.

THE STRESS OF HELPING OR HELPING UNDER STRESS

With very few exceptions, organizations such as hospitals are going through a very critical period in terms of their ability to provide health care. Most people today recognize that organizations operate in a perceived atmosphere of confusion about their role as health care providers. On the one hand, services are available to help people who are injured or unhealthy. On the other hand, the organizations offering these services are blamed when these services fail or lead to compromised patient recovery. Thus health care professionals work in an atmosphere that is charged with the burden of legal responsibilities and the fear of possible malpractice suits. The result is that stress has become synonymous with hospital practice. One of the greatest eye-openers in our careers came when we as professionals, knowing what we did about psychological functioning, took a deeper look at the workings within hospital settings.

HELP FOR THE HELPERS, YESTERDAY AND TODAY

There are two conditions that are necessary before a hospital can begin to effectively eliminate the factors that cripple its ability to offer true health care. The first is that the people in charge, whoever they may be, must recognize to some degree what mental health is and how it relates to the working environment. The second is that they must be willing to promote mental health among the employees in the organization through education. Of the two conditions, the first is crucial because if the decision makers do not know what mental health is, they may very likely do what one hospital did in order to help its employees do a better job. In this hospital, the administrators, to a significant degree, realized that the stressful mental states of their personnel were causing staff and patient problems. The problem was that they did not know what stress was or where it came from. Consequently, they hired a consulting group that subscribed to the belief that all the personnel and patient problems that were being experienced in this hospital resulted primarily from the stress in the environment.

The theme of the hospitalwide program was that health care professionals had to learn techniques to cope with and manage their stress because they were working in an extremely stressful situation. It was stated that stress was inherent in the system, in co-workers, in supervisors, in patients, in low pay, and on and on. Every worker in this hospital was administered a stress test such as those discussed in Chapter 11. Hundreds of people went home the day that psychological inventory was taken with the thought that they were at high risk to have a major physical breakdown due to supposedly stressful events in their lives. One psychologist who took the inventory scored so high that he was told to make sure that he had adequate health insurance. Why? Because he had a new baby, a promotion, a new house, and a new job setting! This, in fact, had been the happiest period of his life!

This situation is commonplace today. There is a prevalent belief that certain settings, events, or conditions are absolutely stressful. Newspaper articles continuously quote mental health professionals who state that a particular job can lead to stress, burnout, even death. Unfortunately, many suggestible workers have accepted such a belief and have fulfilled that unfortunate prophecy.

One of the benefits of realizing the principles presented in this book is that it has clarified for us where such experiences as stress originate. We now know that stress is not inherent in situations, events, or circumstances, and this has made it easier for people to begin to function at healthy levels even in so-called stressful environments such as hospitals. For example, Sharon, a medical secretary, spent several enjoyable hours putting data into a new word processor her department had just bought to facilitate her job. Sharon was thrilled at learning how to use this new tool. She found the work satisfying and pleasurable. However, one afternoon there was a power failure and the data on a disk was lost. In an instant, Sharon felt frustrated and angry at the thought of having to put all the data into the word processor once again. Sharon, however, had learned what negativity meant. She quickly realized that the stress she was feeling was not coming from the work, because obviously she had enjoyed it. Her negative feelings were coming from her thoughts about how unenjoyable it would be to have to do it again. When Sharon dropped these thoughts and simply did the work, she found it to be as enjoyable as it was the first time around. This example shows us that stress is not a result of what we are doing. Rather, stress is a direct result of what we *think* about what we are doing. If we think that we are pressured, hurried, or behind schedule, if we try to do one thing thinking about 20 other things that we think we "should" be doing, then those thinking patterns produce the feelings of stress. Stress is a byproduct of thinking; it is not inherent in situations or circum-stances.

We know that stress is not inherent in work because in any "stressful" job situation there are people who are enjoying what they are doing and working entirely without stress. If the stress were an integral part of the job, everyone would experience it. We have known many intensive-care-unit nurses who work without stress simply by knowing where stress originates. We know nurses and physicians who work in crisis units and emergency rooms with-out experiencing stress.

We have worked with a number of physicians whose lives had become filled with stress. Like many other people in their position, they frequently experienced frustration and anger over such things as nursing problems, inadequate facilities and resources, uncoop-erative patients, burdensome workloads, fear of lawsuits, and in-ter- and intradepartmental disputes. The pet peeve of one physician, a surgeon, was that nonsurgeons were beginning to do colonoscopies, which he considered to be the surgeon's turf. This topic was guaranteed to raise his blood pressure 20 mm of mercury.

When these physicians began to realize that the negative feelings they were experiencing were their own habitual conditioned thoughts about these things, they began dropping these patterns of thinking and their perceptions of their work began to change. With this change in perception, they found it easier to stay out of departmental intrigues. They were more patient and understanding of other people and they, in turn, reciprocated with more positive feelings. They began to produce less negativity, and when they did produce it, their understanding precluded them from blaming it on something external. These professionals were able to utilize their newfound knowledge in their everyday interactions, and they found that common sense and creativity began to emerge in their associates.

These physicians also began to find it easier to leave their medical practice at the hospital so that when they went home, they were able to relax and enjoy their family. All of these positive changes served to increase these physicians' feelings of well-being to an even greater degree. Because of the results that these professionals saw in their work and family life, they realized that the principles were indeed relevant to all areas of their life.

People who have insights into the underlying principles of human psychological functioning have found it easy to reduce or eliminate stress. They find it easier to understand the behaviors of their supervisors, employees, and patients. People with these insights find it easier to avoid creating and perpetuating negative feelings. Nurses with this understanding are able to treat patients with kindness, consideration, patience, and efficiency without reacting to the patient's low state of mind—not because they fear for their job, but out of love for their job. These nurses are able to help patients move into higher states of mind where they perceive and feel more hope and optimism, regardless of their condition. In turn, patients become more relaxed, less anxious, and experience less unnecessary suffering and concern about their condition.

SURGICAL INTENSIVE CARE: A STUDY OF FEELING

In one hospital, we worked with nursing supervisors and staff to help reduce problems that were occurring in an intensive care unit (ICU). As a way of dealing with these problems, the head nurse had developed a whole series of counterproductive control measures. For example, one measure was to require a nurse who had made a medication error to go through a complicated series of demeaning rituals including an investigative committee hearing and extensive paperwork. In addition, a supervisor would periodically follow this person around the ward, looking over her shoulder as she worked. This control measure was not only complicated and inefficient, but it actually served to make the nurse feel more insecure. The supervisor who instituted these measures had no idea that an insecure person who is feeling tense and under stress is much more likely to make an error. This supervisor did not realize that this nurse needed guidance and reassurance to overcome her difficulty. From the beginning, it became clear that the supervisor's frame of reference of how to deal with the situation was itself a major barrier to solving the difficulty and only served to generate more pressure and negativity.

The nursing staff in general was reacting negatively to the rigid control and the pressure from nursing management. This was evidenced by increasing feelings of competitiveness, defensiveness, gossip, absenteeism, and inefficiency. This negativity served to exacerbate the patients' insecurities, thereby eliciting noncompliant and reactive behavior. Overall, it seemed that the problems were unending. They would appear and reappear in a variety of forms, details, issues, events, and situations that involved different combinations of hospital personnel and patients.

It became clear that the people involved in this situation were caught up in a vicious cycle of negative psychological functioning (see figure 4, Chapter 4, page 64) which created negative perceptions, feelings, and behaviors. We realized that the solution to this cycle was twofold. First, we had to help these people to regain some degree of positive feelings (that is, raise their level of consciousness). Second, we had to show them that the source of the negativity was in their own thinking and lack of understanding of thought, rather than attempting to deal with the problematic details that were being generated from that lack of knowledge.

When the staff began to see that they were operating at a low level of mental health, they began to realize that the answer was in raising the overall mood level of the unit. Once the ICU nurses became aware of how insecurities, fears, and biases were connected to low moods and conditioned thinking, they began to make positive changes. They were able to see the common sense in avoiding gossip, reactiveness, and arguments, and the advantages of helping one another. They regained their sense of humor and began looking for ways to make their floor more pleasant. When the nurses began to understand that the patients were being difficult and resistant because they were understandably insecure or frightened, the staff changed their attitude toward the patients who, in turn, became more relaxed, pleasant, optimistic, and cooperative.

As supervisors and nurses became more secure, they felt better and were able to stop exaggerating or dwelling on the details of problems. They found that if they didn't overreact and lose their mental health, they were able to recognize simple, common sense ways of helping their staff rather than just "supervising" them.

With this change in attitude, a general positive feeling began to emerge to replace the we–they feeling that previously existed. People began to realize how easy it was to solve, avoid, or eliminate many of the situations that used to escalate into problems. They learned to be objective, truthful, and yet at the same time, work together to achieve the goals of the ward. The staff began to enjoy their work and their efficiency improved.

The consultation approach that helped this hospital staff was not the teaching of specific techniques such as stress management or communication skills. What many people on this staff realized was that when they were feeling positive, they had no difficulty communicating with each other or with patients. On the other hand, they also realized that when they lost their good feelings they either forgot the technique or they could not make it work. This intervention focused on helping staff understand the psychological common denominators that are involved in everyone's problems. This was accomplished by teaching people the basic principles of human psychological functioning. Once people begin to understand these principles, they are able to see the difference between productive psychological functioning and malfunctioning.

STAFF, HEAL THYSELF

In every instance where the staff has had the courage to look, listen, and learn, problems have been resolved irrespective of how serious the problems may have been. For example, one of the authors worked as a psychologist in the spinal cord injury unit of a hospital. This unit treats adults who have sustained injuries to the spinal cord which have resulted in some degree of paralysis, quadriplegia or paraplegia. Understandably, spinal cord injury is typically accompanied by psychological distress. Initially, many patients are in states of disbelief, depression, or anxiety. Psychologists have assumed that these people will be in a state of trauma or depression for many months and that they will have a difficult time adjusting to their condition.

In an attempt to help these people, the staff of this unit had adopted a treatment model similar to the one many professionals use to help patients adjust to dying. This model holds that a patient must go through stages of denial, anger, depression, and bargaining in order to make a healthy adjustment. Because of this theory, patients would be asked to think about their injuries in such a way that they would experience depression, sadness, grief, and anger. Supposedly, this was to help them face reality. Patients were encourged to dwell on their injuries and express their negative emotions so that these emotions would not be forgotten, "denied," or "repressed" to sneak up at a later date and raise havoc. One therapist spent months struggling with a particular veteran in order to get him to cry nine years after his injury. When she was successful, she claimed to be "exhausted but proud" because she believed that she was helping him "work through" the depression that he had repressed all those years.

The stress associated with trying to help people at this level of understanding was unbelievable. Predictably, this unit was plagued by interpersonal problems and low staff morale. The general atmosphere on the floor was negative—with a high degree of defensiveness, scapegoating, gossip, and general bad feelings between people. Yet major changes began to occur in this unit when a significant number of the staff began to acknowledge and utilize psychological principles and common sense.

As a result, the staff of this unit realized a shift in their level of providing care for their patients. They went from a level of commiseration, as illustrated in figure 9 on page 155 of Chapter 9, to a level of mental health as illustrated in figure 8 on page 145 of Chapter 9. At this level, the staff began to discover that their mental health was the key factor in their ability to do their work and enjoy it without getting caught up in the bad moods of other people. They stopped reacting to negativity and therefore did not feed it or encourage it in any way. The staff began to realize that they could help the patients who were caught up in fears and reactive behavior by not reacting and or commiserating with the patients about how bad or how hopeless things were. The staff could see that this kind of commiserating would keep both staff and patient locked into lower states of mind.

Once the staff began to realize what sanity was and that feelings and emotions are simply indicators of a person's level of mental health, whether it is high (positive feelings) or low (negative feelings), they began to pass this understanding on to patients. The staff began to understand that feelings are created moment to moment through thought, and so they stopped asking patients to think their way out of their predicaments. They began to talk to the patients about what insecurity is and how it is produced. They talked about how feelings of depression, anger, and anxiety are related to thought at a certain level of consciousness, and encouraged patients not to dwell on negative thoughts about their injury or what their life might be in the future.

Once this change occurred in the staff, the new admissions, many of whom were young men in their early 20s, adjusted smoothly and without long periods of agonizing depression. These patients learned what the staff was now demonstrating, that people could have positive feelings that were not contingent on external things. With this understanding, these patients were able to achieve high levels of mental health. They were able to live life with confidence, security, and a sense of humor. They became self-reliant and began to enjoy life. Some patients even went so far as to say that, knowing what they now knew about what feelings are and where they come from, they felt more consistent happiness than they did even before their injury.

With this perspective, it was discovered that 90% to 95% of all the patients were able to make a successful adjustment to their spinal injury without psychological intervention.

AN OVERVIEW

In this chapter we have taken a look at how the principles of human psychological functioning have been utilized in health care settings with excellent results. These results are not isolated or dependent on such factors as personalities, problems, or facilities. When health care professionals know psychological principles, things improve across the board, regardless of the details of the particular situation, because doctors, nurses, lab technicians, social workers, administrators, secretaries, and all other hospital personnel are human beings whose behavior is primarily based on what they think, feel, and perceive. The training that people receive in order to be able to do their jobs does not necessarily have anything to do with finding out what mental health is, how to keep it, or what it even looks like. The health care industry, especially hospitals, will have to recognize this so that it can begin to educate its work force to recognize the connection between their own mental health, their job satisfaction, and their ability to provide *healthy* health care.

For many in the health care professions, work has become a source of stress and aggravation. This sad state of affairs is telling us something if we have the common sense to listen. It is telling us that there is something missing beyond what we presently know as mental health. What we have presented in this book has the potential to fill the gap in our ability as a society to care for ourselves.

In Chapter 4 we noted that our knowledge of mental health has been such that we have considered it something that some people have and others do not, which is why we are not accustomed to recognizing that "normal" people can sometimes lose touch with their mental health. The truth of the matter is that doctors, nurses, psychologists, lab technicians, and other professionals often lose their mental health. It is this lack of mental health, common sense, and understanding, rather than the lack of pertinent skills, that is the cause of most problems in hospitals. We in health care cannot afford to go on blaming our stress and burnout on patients. After all, these are the people who come to us seeking help because we are the ones who promote ourselves as being health care providers. As a society, we already have the technical skills necessary to provide people with excellent health care. What remains to be done is to acquire the sanity necessary to make this fact a reality.

As long as the above fact goes unrecognized, the disrespect, anger, frustration, competition, defensiveness, stress, and burnout seen in hospitals will not be seen for what it is. Instead, we will continue to frustrate ourselves by trying to solve these problems by sending personnel to workshops and seminars that focus on the events and issues resulting from a lack of common sense.

Each moment in a staff's activity can be a step in the direction of health, if the fact of what mental health is is understood. The only limitations in our ability to bring out the health in patients lie in how much mental health we as professionals have realized. Each health care professional, whether a neurosurgeon or a maintenance worker, must learn the common sense necessary to respect his or her own mental health before this respect can be shared with co-workers and patients. Psychologically, to give is to receive. This is why rediscovering the beautiful feelings of excitement and enthusiasm that prompted us to enter a helping profession is to truly find one's reward—sanity.

CHAPTER FIFTEEN

Breaking Through Thought

The field of psychology as a whole is now spawning more and more divergent theories and techniques, many of which are contradictory in their treatment methods; yet all conform within the context of certain basic assumptions about the effects of our pasts and our limited ability to change our minds. This proliferation of theories and techniques is a sign of the field's frustration in trying to break through to an answer, but not knowing that this cannot occur within the context of existing basic assumptions. The field of psychology will begin to move ahead as it realizes that it has been focusing on the effect of thought, rather than thought itself.

Today's psychology, as a collection of theories, concepts, and techniques, has attempted to help people and society realize relief from mental problems via methods that do nothing to increase one's understanding of the role and power of thought. This has led to the misperception that rituals, techniques, or other placebos are the route to change. Thus, by creating the illuson of change through altering the form or format through which people express their insecurity, negative feelings, and dependencies, psychology has unwittingly contributed to its own inability to progress as a science and as a field. There is nothing to be found in studying and in explaining the attributes of placebo sugar pills, water injections, or psychotherapeutic rituals because in the end it is the human being's level of understanding and ability to think that brings results.

For example, during the late 1700s, the phenomenon associated with what is today known as hypnosis, involving compliance or suggestibility, was thought by Austrian physician Friedrich Anton Mesmer and others to be due to animal magnetism (treatment with the use of magnets), which was an available concept of the times. Later, these same results were attributed to a specific ritual or "hypnotic induction" (watching a pendulum or waving a time-piece). Then, it was noted that the induction procedures were not the point. That is, the same level of compliance thought to require hypnosis could be achieved without any "hypnotic induction" whatsoever. Most recently, psychologists have begun to realize that hypnosis involves tapping into the subject's existing expectations and that there is really no such thing as a "trance." This is what was being demonstrated in the study cited in Chapter 10 which compared hypnotized and non-hypnotized subjects. It was found that the level of compliance normally associated with being in a "hypnotic trance" was present in all subjects in the form of "demand characteristics," and was even more strongly manifested by the non-"hypnotized" subjects than with those who were supposedly in a hypnotic trance. There are present-day authorities in the mental health field who are beginning to realize that hypnosis is a placebo effect that depends on the beliefs and expectations of the individual. What is another word for expectations? Thought. So, in understanding extreme cases of compliance, we in psychology have gone from animal magnetism to hypnotic rituals to placebos, and now, to thought.

ANOMALIES OR ANSWERS?

When astronomers believed that the earth was the center of the universe, all studies of the stars and planets were carried out within this frame of reference. At this level, astronomy was not able to even explain the alternation of night and day! In an attempt to explain its lack of results, the field became diverse and spawned a variety of different theories and models. When Copernicus came up with the notion that the earth was not the center of the uni-verse and that the planets, including the earth, revolved around the sun, this idea was seen as heresy. Martin Luther, Copernicus's contemporary, is reputed to have stated, "The fool wants to turn the whole science of astronomy upside down." Yet, in the long run, the compelling logic of this new idea was too much for astronomers to resist. It even explained the mystery of night and day. In hindsight, it is now obvious that the barrier to these new ideas was one of thought; a barrier erected by our own ignorance in insisting on maintaining a view of reality rather than seeking an answer.

Similarly, before Einstein laid out the principles of relativity, the clues were building up within the research of the field of physics. Phenomena had been observed and measured that did not fit together easily without creating forced and complicated explanations given the frame of reference of underlying assumptions of Newtonian physics. But for a long time, no one could see that these exceptions to the established rules were the clues to a more profound understanding. In both astronomy and physics, then, there had been an increasing number of clues popping up in the research and observations up to that time which had been ignored or distorted to fit the existing frame of reference. What constituted a breakthrough was when someone saw that all these anomalies added up to an answer that brought in a new reality, one characterized by more integration, simplicity, and clarity.

The studies, illustrations, and anecdotes that we have cited in this book are not just stories, they are realities that are being experienced by millions of people day in and day out. The object now is to begin to look at these clues, not through the filters of what we, as mental health professionals, think we already know, but to look with no preconceptions, with no set ideas about any relationship or pattern that we bring with us. We must approach these observations with a new openness that allows us to see the logic or principle that emerges from their implications.

After a significant shift in the level of understanding of any field, it is possible to look back and see that the implications for that new direction had been there all along. But the reason why these implications were not recognized is that they were seen as anomalies rather than answers. The barrier which always stands in the way is that the implications pointing to a new framework are always one step removed from the details in the existing frame of reference. We must remember, however, that even when someone gets a glimpse of the new level of understanding, there is an attempt to validate that glimpse using the concepts with which we are familiar. It is, however, impossible to prove the new using the old frame of reference.

For example, when we first began to recognize the principles of the Psychology of Mind, we saw it as something to incorporate into the context of how we were already approaching psychotherapy and teaching. Yet as our exploration in this direction proceeded, we realized that everything else we were doing was a manifestation or demonstration of the degree to which people understood the principle of thought. As a result, we abandoned our old beliefs, views, and approaches and began to realize a whole new level of psychology.

It seems that it is time for the field to break through this barrier in order to realize a higher step in the evolution of our understanding of the mind. The next step is to realize that the power to change lies not in the specific details of a person's beliefs, but in understanding the power to think. What will begin to be recognized within the mental health profession is that the actual power which gives life to all conditioned illusions, including such illusions as the placebo effect, is available directly to people without need for a middleman or mediating agent.

What we are saying about the present status quo of psychology has nothing to do with the rightness or wrongness of any specific theory, therapeutic ritual, or process. What we are saying is that all of the traditional theories and approaches that exist today are a result of a context that was configured by people who had no understanding of thought as presented in this book. This context, in the form of assumptions and beliefs commonly held by the field today, has gone unquestioned and, thus, continues to dominate the perceptions of the mental health professional. So much so, that if an alcoholic is cured, a traditionalist will state that that individual was not really an alcoholic because "alcoholics," by their definition, can never be cured. Similarly, anyone who recovers from schizophrenia, manic depressive disorder, or the like is considered to not have been suffering from those disorders. Recently compulsive gambling and compulsive shopping have been added to the list of "diseases" that are beyond will power to control and for which there exists no cure. Yet, there are many people who do realize a cure for these disorders. Up until now, however, the field has been so steeped in the reality of its own thinking that instead of looking at these results as answers, it dismisses them as exceptions to the rules—anomalies!

BEYOND TECHNIQUES

One major ramification of realizing the principles of the Psychology of Mind is that it has changed our definition of what is therapeutic. We now see more clearly that techniques, activities, or behaviors and specific rewards we place around people are not necessarily therapeutic. The term *therapeutic* implies the restoration of health. Many rituals that are labeled therapeutic will be abandoned. Techniques, which attempt to change a client's emotional state without the understanding of the client, will be used less and less once the deeper nature of the irresponsibility of these methods is seen more clearly. Therapists will move away from a reliance on therapeutic techniques and rituals and will begin to direct people toward the understanding emerging from a recognition of the principles of thought, separate realities, feelings, and levels of consciousness.

Perhaps the most important shift will be that the health of the helper will be seen as the key variable. That is, instead of a theory or a technique, the quality of feelings and level of understanding in the therapist will become the recognized source of guidance in psychotherapy.

Beyond this, we will start to see the antitherapeutic quality of tying people to their problems, their past, their personalities, and their diagnoses. Rather than looking for more detailed descriptions of types or categories of problems and sources of discomfort or bad habits, psychology will begin to impersonalize the psychological dynamics that keep people recycling distorted thought patterns, the thoughts of insecurity. Therapy will be turned more toward uncovering or drawing out people's inherent understanding, common sense, and wisdom, and moving away from a problem-oriented search for solutions, and a destructive labeling of patients as diseased in some way. In return, the results that psychology now seeks will become evident as we, our clients, families, and society begin to manifest an overall greater degree of mental health, happiness, and creativity.

Psychology, as a science, will then begin to look in an opposite direction from where it is searching now, straight to a deeper understanding of the impersonal principles of how psychological functioning operates moment to moment to create an experience of whatever is going on at the time. As we begin to understand what mental health is, we will also begin to realize that there are deeper, or higher, degrees of mental health potentially accessible to people. The most exciting research will not be focused on mental distress at all but will explore, through our own deepening common sense, the higher levels of consciousness available to us as human beings.

With this understanding, the field will begin to see the common principles pointed to by the various forms of consciousness or awareness disciplines that have emerged from other cultures. We will begin to see what aspects of these disciplines are psychologically valid across cultures. In this way, the mental health professional will be able to identify the impersonal essence or principles involved in these systems so as to be able to relate them to this society in a more direct and common-sense manner. This will allow people to realize their practical benefits without becoming entangled in the trappings of a foreign culture, lifestyle, dogma, and the accompanying rituals of each conceptualization.

The field of psychology will take a new and exciting direction when we begin to look directly toward the mental power we as human beings possess. Once this new wisdom is shared with people, the benefits will spill over to society to help many people who are now looking for relief from emotional distress, from their own fears and anxiety, from mental illness and a recurrent life of self-destructive behaviors that always seem just out of individual control.

This direction is also the one that will help the most people in the long run because, whether we are talking about improving the quality of our own individual reality or that of a society or even an entire humanity, the principle is the same and the only barriers to accomplishing these feats are those of thought. It is the knowledge of this fact that will allow human beings to successfully break the perceptual, emotional, and behavioral barriers of life.

CHAPTER SIXTEEN

The Emergence
of a New
Understanding
of the
Mind

Albert Einstein once stated, "The world we have made as a result of the level of thinking we have done thus far, creates problems we cannot solve at the same level at which we created them." When Sigmund Freud presented his beliefs about human psychological functioning to the world, the knowledge of thought was, for all practical purposes, nonexistent. The societal level of understanding was too low to afford the people of that time any immunity from such beliefs. Consequently, Freud's thoughts were taken seriously. They were accepted by the healer as a tool with which to help people find their sanity. Freud's thoughts about people's personality, his ideas of the unshakable power of the past and of the necessity of ritualistically analyzing the details of one's problems, and his notion that people were fundamentally psychically flawed or unhealthy created a psychological context for the field of mental health. The frame of reference that Freud was speaking from is still, in one form or another, the basis for trying to help people find their mental health today.

Since Freud, theorist after theorist has offered his or her description of the psychological maze of life as they see it, along with directions for how to cope with living in this maze. But no matter how precise the descriptions, all have missed the fact that life, as a perception, originates in thought. No one has recognized that the maze is thought-created. Human beings live in the reality of their own thought-created perceptions, and it is the degree of understanding of this fact that determines whether or not they will be imprisoned in their own world. The very birth of psychology was the first glimmer of the fact that life is lived from the inside out rather than from the outside in. The principles of the Psychology of Mind are the embodiment of this glimmer.

No one can say that Freud was wrong in the manner in which

he experienced human functioning. Rather, we are talking about the evolution of *our* understanding of how the mind works so that we can rise above all the misconceptions that were generated because of a lack of understanding of how people's experience in life is created. At one point in history, for example, healers thought that people with certain symptoms were possessed by demons and that physical illness was caused by bad blood. Because of the level of understanding that prevailed at that time, these ideas were seen as legitimate, as a result, people were exorcised, tortured, burned, or drowned as witches, and indiscriminent bloodletting was a common medical treatment. Since that time, we as a humanity have come a long way in understanding how the body functions. By comparison, however, our knowledge of our own mental workings has progressed only minutely, as reflected in the fact that Freud's level of thinking persists as a legitimate way to treat people experiencing mental problems. We cannot blame Freud's thoughts because we lacked the understanding to see beyond them. But, once we have understanding, we will also have the courage and integrity to look beyond such beliefs, recognize their total invalidity, and understand why so many people accept them.

For centuries, humanity has attempted to understand its own psychological functioning by utilizing as a tool the products of the very functioning it seeks to understand. Thus scientists have tried to understand people's behavior from within the confines of their own theoretical beliefs and perceptions. The content of human thought, in fact, became the standard by which the mental health professional has measured, gauged, and understood human behavior. However, what we have discovered and tried to convey in this book is that the content of each human being's thoughts is far more unique than what any social scientist has fathomed, and furthermore, that using thought content as a vehicle of understanding human behavior has led to increased misunderstanding between people's realities.

In the course of our studies we realized that there is no answer to the psychological riddle within those boundaries of the contents of thought. Rather, the answer lies one psychological step beyond the specific realm of details in a deeper level of understanding. This deeper answer involves realizing the principles of what the mind is and how it functions to generate individual and cultural realities made up of specific details, beliefs, values, opinions, attitudes, perceptions, and behaviors. This new "tool" that has been realized is not an external device, belief system, or ritual, but a realization of an understanding that exists at a deeper level of consciousness than the contents of our thinking. One step before thinking, a psychological realm of mind, one that is truly objective, exists. This realm is a level of consciousness that is as accessible as the air we breathe.

A cardinal aspect of the Psychology of Mind is that it clarifies how, in the absence of understanding thought, both individuals or groups such as sciences and cultures will become "stuck" within the confines of problem-oriented ways of seeing reality without knowing that they are experiencing the end product of their thinking. The intervals between great discoveries or changes are characterized by a growing dependence on certain fixed ideas and views, in a manner that inhibits change. As a result, humanity has periodically had to struggle to free itself from its own outdated ideas in order to advance its understanding. In this respect, the field of mental health has been no different in terms of the maze of theories through which it attempts to help people.

In the first chapter of this book we posed some important questions that arise from the anomalies in such studies as "On Being Sane in Insane Places." What are the costs to a society when its mental health experts are not only unable to recognize or diagnose mental health, but are predisposed to perceive the sane as being insane? To what degree are our traditional treatment approaches unknowingly promoting insanity? To what degree are the problems of our society a direct or indirect result of our inability to see mental health when it is present? What would be the potential benefits to society if we were to realize such mastery? In other words, what would happen if the field of psychology were to become a more exact science?

The answers to the first three questions are straightforward. What we as mental health professionals have been experiencing is the realistic forms of our own level of understanding, our own thoughts that shape our perceptions of people. Without knowing it, we have been wrestling with our own misperceptions of life in the same way that people, sciences, cultures, and societies have had to wrestle with their misconceived views of reality. This explains why the traditional psychotherapist, in an effort to help people change, innocently tells people over and over again, in many different ways, how fundamentally unhealthy they are or how much they are products of their pasts and prisoners of their innate psychic conflicts, their habits and styles, and how difficult it is to change any of these. Like the psychotherapists treating George, we have been wrestling with our own misconceptions of thought without knowing it. Many of society's problems, whether at the level of an individual problem (stress, anxiety, depression) or at the group level (social disorder, poverty, wars), stem from our own inability to see this connection.

The answer to the last two questions is also straightforward. We are on the brink of something that is as beautiful as it is unthinkable. We are on the brink of finding out what happens when a society begins to discover that common sense, wisdom, love, understanding, compassion, and so forth are words that describe the same thing, *mental health.* To date, mental health has been considered to be something possessed by some but not all. Our most recent realization is that mental health is something that is possessed by every human being. Furthermore, the means of drawing out this innate resource can be described.

In this book we have provided an introduction to this new psychology, the Psychology of Mind, and its basic principles in order to point the way toward a higher level of understanding in the field of psychology. Based on a recognition of the role of thought in creating our realities, this new direction will lead us out of the problem-oriented realities which we experience as human beings.

The birth of a "new idea" is only the beginning. The idea must mature into a reality. Our evolution as human beings, as a science, and as a helping profession will emerge with greater degrees of our mental health. Our evolution will emerge as a willingness to accept something new, to listen to someone saying that the world is round rather than flat; that the earth is not the center of the solar system; that energy, matter, and space are related, or that perhaps by shifting our focus away from the manifestations of people's problems to the principles of thought, reality, consciousness, and emotions we will see our connection to mental health. The simplicity of this new psychology has given us the means of helping people realize a cure for conditions that have been considered incurable. What this means to a society is that it has found the route to its own wisdom.

NOTES

CHAPTER 1. The Nature of Science and the Field of Mental Health

1. Rosenhan, D. L. (1973). On being sane in insane places. *Science, 179,* 250–258.

2. Corsini, R. (Ed.). (1981). *Handbook of innovative psychotherapies.* New York: McGraw-Hill.

3. Turner, P. (1986). The shrinking of George. *Science 86,* (June), 38–44.

4. Frank, J. D. (1961). *Persuasion and healing: A comparative study of psychotherapy* pp. 15–16. Baltimore: Johns Hopkins University Press.

5. London, I. & Thorngate, W. (1981). Divergent amplification and social behavior: Some methodological considerations. *Psychological Reports, 48,* 203–228.

6. Einstein, A., & Infeld, L. (1938). *The evolution of physics* (p. 259). New York: Simon & Schuster.

7. *Ibid.,* p. 287.

CHAPTER 10. The Need for an Advanced Psychology: Toward a Deeper Understanding

1. Milgram, S. (1983). Behavioral study of obedience. *Journal of Abnormal and Social Psychology, 67,* 371–378.

2. Orne, I., & Evans, F. (1965). Social control in the psychological experiment: Antisocial behavior and hypnosis. *Journal of Personality and Social Psychology, 1,* 189–200.

3. Rosenthal, R. (1966). *Experimental effects in behavioral research.* New York: Appleton Century-Crofts.

CHAPTER 11. Today's Psychology in Theory: A Level of Consciousness

1. Velikovsky, I. (1950). *Worlds in collision.* New York: Macmillan.

2. Mahoney, M. J. (1976). *Scientist as subject* (pp. 116–117). Cambridge, MA: Ballinger.

3. Jeffrey, R. (1964). The psychologist as an expert witness on the issue of insanity. *American Psychologist, 19,* 838–843.

4. United States v. Kent, No. 798–61, District Court for the District of Columbia.

5. United States v. Jenkins, No. 614–59, District Court for the District of Columbia.

CHAPTER 12. A Perspective on Traditional Psychotherapies

1. Prioleaux, L., Murdock, M., & Brody, N. (1983). An analysis of psychotherapy versus placebo studies. *The Behavioral and Brain Sciences, 6,* 275–310.

CHAPTER 13. Application of Psychological Principles to Organizations

1. Homans, G. C. (1965). Group factors in worker productivity. In H. Proshansky & L. Seidenberg (Eds.), *Basic studies in psychology* (pp. 592–604). New York: Holt.

INDEX

Accomplishments, and insecurity, 83
Activated thought system, 30
Anomalies
  studies as, 6
  value of, 6
Anxiety, and insecurity, 80

Behavioral experiments, contamination of research, 163–64
Behavior therapies, basis/focus of, 202–3
Belief systems
  beliefs and thoughts, 25, 28, 30, 32
  conversion process, 116, 127
  frames of reference, 116
Burnout, 50
  of therapists, 152, 154
    avoidance of, 154

Change
  power of thought and, 29–30, 35, 38
    case study, 36–38
  psychological barriers to, 80
  shift to higher level of consciousness, 45–46, 47
Cognitive therapy
  basic assumption, 203
  first-generation of, 203–4
  needs for, 204–5
  techniques used, 204
  value of, 204
Commiseration versus compassion, by therapist, 152–56
Common sense, 59–61
  explanation of concept, 59–60
  insecurity and, 76

Common sense (cont.)
  versus intelligence, 192–93
  in organizations, 221
  as positive view of reality, 60
Compatibility, love relationships, 86
Concepts, conditioned nature of, 165–67
Conditioning
  by products of, attention to, 162–63
  conditioned nature of concepts/theories, 165–67
  illusory nature of, 162
  Pavlov's discovery, 161–62
Consciousness, See Levels of consciousness.
Contamination, psychological experiments, 163–64
Conversion process, belief systems, 116, 127
Coping methods, for insecurity, 76–77
Counselors, See Therapists; Therapist's role.

Demand characteristics, psychological experiments, 164, 165
Drive, and insecurity, 83

Ego
  and change, 97–102
  and conflict, 102
  definition/explanation of, 95–96
  dropping attachment to ego, 99, 100–101
  happiness and, 101

277

Index

279

Index

Index

Index

Index

Index

Thought (*cont.*)
    and mental health, 68–69
    perceptions/feelings/behavior and, 30, 32
    screening process, 25–26
    theories as product of, 166–67
    thought and reality, 26, 29
    usefulness of, 110–11

Velikovsky, Immanuel, rejection of, 177–78
Verbal intelligence, 191

Well-adjusted people, 147

Wisdom
    beginning of, 110
    characteristics of, 107–8, 111–12
    and insight, 109–10, 111–12
    intellectualization as barrier to, 148–49
    jigsaw puzzle example, 112
    and mental health, 108–9
    as psychological factor, 109
    versus realism, 110
    unconditioned frame of reference, 117–20
Worry, and insecurity, 84

ABOUT THE AUTHORS

Dr. Rick Suarez and *Dr. Roger C. Mills* were introduced to each other at a psychology conference in 1979. Their meeting resulted in the new Psychology of Mind. In 1981 the Advanced Human Studies Institute was established in Coral Gables, Florida, to serve as a major clinical, research and training center for the new psychology. With Dr. Suarez as its Executive Director, the Institute operates as a nonprofit center providing individual and group psychotherapy, marriage and family counseling, substance abuse and stress counseling. The Institute offers predoctoral and postgraduate training for health-care professionals, therapists, educators, and business managers. *Darlene Stewart* is a therapist and Assistant Director at the Institute. All have families and live in the Greater Miami area.